Tina and Lou w
God is always wi.
a magnificent journey that your soul will one day take. Their vivid description of her near death experience and what she encounters will leave you uplifted and with a renewed spirit. *The Journey* reassures that God has a plan for everybody, you just have to trust that He will guide you along your path.

Kary Oberbrunner, author of Your Secret Name and
The Elixer Project

As a mother of four sons who now live in Heaven, reading through Tina's story *The Journey* made me feel closer to my boys. The description of Heaven through her words, made eternity come even more alive in my heart. The colors of heaven are so beautifully described in her artwork. If you have a loved one already there or just have any doubts about the world to come this book is a must read.

Debra Lynn Hayes, author of RISE....What To Do When
Hell Won't Back Off

The Journey is a must read for anyone who has pondered their relationship with God and His divine plan. Life beyond this Earthly realm as described by Tina and Lou Bouris includes family ties throughout the generations, eternal beauty beyond description, and a bond with our Heavenly Father that has existed since the beginning of time. The Journey is a faith builder, reaffirming the worth of the individual in God's eyes and giving strength to make it through our unique journey of life.

Nanette O'Neal, author of *A Doorway Back to Forever:
Believe.*

A genuine and touching story that pulls at your heartstrings. *The Journey* is a truly unique and colorful tapestry that will not only give you a different perspective on this life, but also what's to come.

Melissa Kuo, Owner of Copperloch Antiques and
Galleria LLC

THE
JOURNEY

THE JOURNEY

My Near Death Experience to Heaven and Back

TINA AND LOU BOURIS

Published by Author Academy Elite
P.O. Box 43 Powell, OH 43035
www.AuthorAcademyElite.com

Paperback ISBN: 978-1-64085-132-0

Hardback ISBN: 978-1-64085-136-8

Ebook ISBN: 978-1-64085-137-5

For my mom, who taught me how to pray

For my Baba, who taught me how to listen

For my sisters Angela and Anita, for always being there for me.

For my husband Lou, for going on this Journey with me and giving my story a voice.

A special thank you to Gary Price for pulling me out of the water and saving my life. My Journey was made possible because of you.

And especially for God, who is always with me, guiding me through my Journey.

PROLOGUE

Usually when people talk about the best day of their life, they reminisce about their first kiss, their wedding day, or the birth of their children. I will never forget the events of the greatest day of my life. It was the day that I learned that my life was not as small and insignificant as I once thought. The day when I learned what true, unconditional love was. It was the day that I realized that everybody possessed within themselves something special.

It was the day that I died.

PART 1...

I t was my favorite time of the year. The leaves had just about fully turned, with fiery oranges and reds exploding from all of the trees. A bright sun and a crispness in the air reminds me how great it is to be alive. This was what I liked to call a sweatshirt and sunglasses type of day.

Lou would be there soon, but I figured I'd go early to spend some time alone with Nature. Being in the fresh air rejuvenated me, gave me a sense of calm that I didn't get anywhere else.

Simply put, Nature was my spiritual church.

To me, there really wasn't much difference between being spiritual and being religious. Both are praising God and giving thanks for all that He has given to us—they simply go about it in a slightly different way. When I was outside in Nature, it fed my spiritual side. I saw all of His creations, and appreciated how significant life is on this planet. I could literally see and feel God's creations at work.

Being religious? I would say it's almost like 'organized spirituality.' I know I'm a deeply religious person at heart, so it's not that I didn't believe in going to church or that there were no benefits from attending a church on Sundays, but there were times I felt so much closer to God out here amongst the trees. I understand the Bible states you need to congregate with others and pray, and I believe in that as well. For years I used to get up early on Sunday and my grandparents would pick me up in order to go to church with them. Even though my parents owned their own business and worked every weekend, I don't think I'd ever missed a Sunday church service. Not gonna lie though, at times I really enjoyed the church service, but at other times I felt like I was there because I was supposed to be. I couldn't disappoint my grandparents, so I had to make sure I was ready to go and in our same seats before church started.

Now that I'm older and living out on my own, I don't quite make it to church as often as I probably should. I still get a lot out it when I do go, but I'm also finding that sleeping in late on a Sunday morning is pretty spiritual in itself. Getting up early and working all week, seems to take a toll on me. Combine that with all the medication I'm taking now, it seems almost impossible to get up in time for church, especially when I know I can sleep as late as I think my body needs.

Maybe if I did force myself to wake up early and go to church more often, then I would have met Lou a little earlier. He's one of the good church-going guys that my grandmother said I should always try to find, the kind that she would always say is right in front of you—you just have to keep your eyes and mind open.

Well, he might not have been right in front of me, but if I would have gone to church more often, he would've been right behind me. Close enough, right?

My grandparents always sat in the same pew at church every Sunday. In fact, everybody always sat in the same seats—very few would ever dare to deviate from the norm. The little old Greek ladies would definitely be all-abuzz if, God forbid, somebody came in and had the nerve to sit in one of their seats!

That's why my grandmother knew that I would eventually run into Lou. His family always sat right behind her and my grandfather, so it was just a matter of time before we would both be at church at the same time. When we finally met up outside of church to hang out and talk, her and her friends began to gossip like little schoolgirls.

"Just keep things light." She would tell me. "Don't scare him away with your crazy story!"

"Come on Yia-Yia," which is Greek for grand-mother, "My story is what makes me who I am. I'm not going to hide anything. If it comes up, which it probably will, then I'll see what he has to say about it and just go from there."

"All the boys you tell that crazy story to look at you differently afterwards and are gone before you ever go out with them again." She always told me.

"Yeah, well then I guess they weren't the right ones then. If somebody can't handle my story, then they can't handle being with me," I would tell her defiantly.

Well, I guess I'd find out soon enough. Lou saun-tered into the clearing where I told him I would meet him, waving and heading my way.

* * *

"Wow, this place is amazing." Lou said glancing around at all the incredible scenery.

I took a step off the path and into the grassy field, arms stretched out with my face looking straight up into the sunny sky spinning around for dramatic effect.

"Welcome to my church away from church!" I told him. "The beautiful colors in the trees are like my stained glass windows with a view straight to heaven. I always feel close to God when I'm out here."

"Yeah, I can tell." Lou laughed as I kept spinning around. "You seem like you've got a pretty good relationship with the Big Guy."

"Now? Yeah, I guess you could say that. But it wasn't always this way. There was a time in my life that I *really* questioned God."

"Well there's always a time in every Christian's life where they kind of question things, right? I mean, who hasn't had a rough patch as a kid or something?"

I stopped spinning and looked sheepishly down at my shoes as Lou said that. I felt my cheeks getting warm with apprehension. We had only been out on this walk a few minutes and we were already heading right down the path to my "crazy story," as my grandmother would say. Guess I shouldn't be too surprised, we met at church … we're talking about Nature and God … of course it would circle right down that path.

"Yeah, well when you're only a little kid and you find out you have some strange illness that you've never heard of before, and you realize you're going to have it for the rest of your life and there's nothing you or anybody can do about ... well, you tend to not only get really angry at God, but question his existence altogether."

PART 2...

"It actually kind of started right here in this park. I mean, this is the place where I first realized there might have been something wrong with me."

"So you found out that you were sick when you were little? Are you still sick? I mean, you don't—"

"Look sick?" I finished his sentence for him and laughed. "Yeah, I know. I hear that *all* the time. I've got epilepsy. Right around here was the first time it made its presence known in my life."

"So you have seizures and stuff like that? I know what epilepsy is, but I don't think I've ever seen anybody have a seizure. Did you have one here in this park when you were here with your school?" The seriousness on Lou's face was unmistakable, and his piercing stare seemed to reach straight to my soul. He looked legitimately concerned at this point.

"There are a couple of different types of seizures. When we were here learning about nature and all the animals that live in this area, I zoned out. At least I thought at the time I just zoned out. I had a snake around my neck, just a small one that lives near the

7

creek that the ranger was talking about, and I can remember enjoying the feel of it and the coolness on my neck. Then out of nowhere I seem to have completely forgotten that it was on me, and I jumped back and threw it to the ground. It was like I was completely gone for a few seconds, and when I came back to reality, I didn't know what was going on."

"So you just completely lost time. You were here but not really," he concluded.

"Yep. Turns out it was a small seizure, called a petit mal. That's one of the types of seizures epileptics have. You don't really hear about them much, but they really rob you of time. It might look like I am just spacing out, but in actuality it's a form of a small seizure. It's like time jumps forward without you, and you miss everything that's going on around you while you're in this type of trance. Now, the really big seizures are the scary ones. That's the type you probably think of when you hear about an epileptic getting sick. Right?"

"Yeah, exactly. Gran Maul I think they're called. You have those too?" The concerned look on his face grew even more as he gently put his hand on my back and guided me down a slight slope in the trail. I couldn't tell if he was nervous about my stories of having seizures as a kid or if he was worried if I could possibly have one while we were out here on our little hike.

"Not often, but yes those are a part of this illness as well. The one that set my life on the track it is happened on what was supposed to be a fun family outing. We all had gone to an amusement park. After getting off a ride with my sister and friend, it hit me hard. Apparently I'd just started drifting away from my sister while she was talking to me, and then I stood there and stared, kind of like the little ones. I vaguely remember that, but afterward, everything had gone blank. Don't recall anything that happened next, but it was something that Angie would never forget. I had dropped to my knees and just started shaking and convulsing. I'd lost control of everything, and I do mean everything—including my bladder," I said, trying to soften the embarrassing blow of telling your date that you peed all over yourself.

Lou came to an abrupt halt, stopping dead in his tracks and seemingly unwilling, or unable, to look up from the rock that he was kicking through the dust.

"Man, that had to be unbelievably scary for your sister. Especially since there was no warning or anything, you just dropped and had a seizure."

"And to make matters worse, people were actually watching and laughing at me. They thought I was just peeing my pants because the 'ride was too scary' for an eight year old little girl like me. Angie kept yelling at everyone, trying to help me—but she really had no idea what to do."

We walked in silence for the a few minutes, looking around at the scenery and more than likely trying to figure out what the other was thinking. I glanced over at him a few times as we approached another small creek, trying to gage exactly what he was thinking.

"That must have been so tough for you," He said it so lightly I barely heard him. "So, did they just know right away it was epilepsy because of that big seizure?" he asked, breaking the silence that we were sharing.

9

"Well, they did a bunch of testing. My dad and sister went with me to the hospital and they did blood work, EEG, CAT scan, trying to get a gage on what was going on with my brain. I hated it. But you know what? Although I had endured seizures and monster migraines afterward, I'm not sure who it was harder on—me or my family."

"Really? How is that even possible if you're the one going through all that mess?" Lou asked.

His question hit me hard. If there was one thing I had learned growing up with a disorder like epilepsy, it's that although you might feel isolated while you're having seizures, it really takes its toll on your entire family. When I had to stay up all night for my first EEG, my entire family had stayed up with me playing video games and telling stories to make sure I stayed awake. I can still remember how nervous my dad and sister were when they went with me to get all those tests done. When we were at home, my parents were afraid to leave me alone for fear that I would have another seizure and there'd be nobody there to help. I couldn't take a shower without somebody sitting in the bathroom to make sure I was fine. Even my little sister, the girl that I was supposed to help look after, kept "an eye on me" when we would play together. Every aspect of my family's life changed, and I was the reason. But the biggest way it affected them, the one that I'll never be able to get out of my mind, was the way they looked at me after I had a seizure.

The uneasiness.

The fear.

The look that they were scared to death, and they knew that there was nothing they could do for their little girl. They tried to smile and tell me everything was going to be fine, and that I was going to eventually be okay.

But I knew.

I knew how much it hurt them when I came out of a seizure, and had no idea where I was. When I would look at each of them directly in the eye and would have no idea who they were. My memory always came back in a minute or so, but for those precious seconds the people who loved me the most were complete strangers to me.

I felt a shiver run through me as I slightly turned away from him. I could sense the tears slowly welling up, trying to escape my eyes. Keeping my head turned I wiped away the solitary tear that made its way to my cheek before I continued.

"I might have been the one that had the seizures, but it affected everyone. You have no idea what it feels like to be the weakest link in the family."

"You survived all that and you're still standing, so you can't be that much of a weak link. I've never had any of those tests. EEG, CAT scan, those had to have been traumatic for someone so young. Especially since you really didn't know what was going on with your brain. How did they go?

"The EEG was the worse. I had to be sleep deprived in order for them to get a good reading on my brainwaves. But what I didn't know was what they had to do to actually get those readings. Once I was all wired up, they told me to just lie down and relax, and that it would be just fine if I fell asleep."

My stomach tightened up just thinking of how these tests actually made me feel.

"Well, that doesn't sound too bad of a test."

"Yeah, well as soon as I closed my eyes and was just about to doze off, the room seemed to fill with flashing lights. At first I thought it was my brain misfiring again and causing me to see things. I then realized this was part of the test. They basically had a strobe light going off in the room trying to trigger something in my brain."

"Wow, that doesn't sound good. What happened? Did it trigger anything? You get sick?"

"Oh yeah. I felt that tingle in my brain again, then nothing. The only thing I remembered was trying to open my eyes, and then trying to figure out where I was and who the people were standing around my bed."

"So they *wanted* you to have a seizure? That sounds pretty harsh. You really had no idea what happened or where you were?" He shook his head in disbelief, and I could really see the concern growing on his face with each question.

"They said that if I had seizure activity while I was all hooked up with the wires, they would get a good reading. There's a small percentage of epilepsy patients that have a sensitivity to flashing lights, and this was their way of testing for that. And if by chance I had that, which I obviously did, then they would be able to see what parts of my brain were misfiring during a seizure. I guess you could say it was win-win for them on that front. I was extremely sensitive to the lights, which gave them a great reading on the EEG.

"When I would come out of a seizure, it was almost like coming out of a weird fog. Everything was fuzzy, and I had no memory whatsoever of what had just happened. I wouldn't know where I was, and I normally had no idea who anybody was. Friends, doctors, family members, it didn't matter who they were. If I saw them as soon as I was out of 'seizure mode,' I would have no clue who they were. After a few minutes, I would be able to remember everybody, and I also would remember exactly what I went through. Although that's normally not anything that you really want to remember if you ask me."

Lou was really into it. "When you had your seizure during that EEG session, you said your dad and sister were at the hospital with you. Did they see you have that seizure? No way they were in the room with you, right?"

"No, obviously they couldn't be in there with me, but right before I laid back and closed my eyes, I could see him through a small window in the door. I couldn't see my sister. She must have been sitting in the waiting room somewhere. But I could see my dad grinning at me and waving wildly with both hands. He looked more nervous than I was, but I knew he was trying to take my mind off what was going on. Of course, neither of us realized what they were doing, but I loved the way he was trying to cheer me up."

"He knew how scared I was, and he did his best that whole day to try to make me laugh and get me to forget about what was going on. At least as much as he could. He said how cool it was to get the CAT scan, that I would be the only person we knew with an actual picture of my brain. Maybe they would let us take it home and he would frame it and hang it in the living room by the fireplace." I laughed remembering all of my dad's antics that day trying to get me to smile. Looking back on that day now, I realize just how hard it had to have been for him. I tried not to cry too much or complain throughout the testing, but it couldn't have been easy to see me get poked and prodded that whole time.

We walked in silence for a bit again. I started feeling a little self-conscious with all this talk about me and my sickness. It normally doesn't bother me much. People ask all the time about epilepsy and how I found out that I had it. I could talk about it to anyone, and I like getting the word out about the disease. It's one that a lot of people suffer from, but not that many people actually know much about. The more I talk about it the more people know.

"Okaaay," I said a little sheepishly, "you're hearing a ton about me and what's wrong with my head. You're probably getting a little tired of all this woe-is-me talk."

"If there's one thing I am learning about you, it's that you definitely do *not* have a *woe-is-me* attitude. If anything, I would think you'd take something like that head-on and fight your way through it, right? You and God versus this strange, evil disorder!"

"Ha, far from it. I would say it was almost the exact opposite of that. Becoming a teenager is hard enough, and I had to do it handicapped with this stupid disease? I was not in a good place at that time. Me and God versus epilepsy? More like Me versus God." I was almost embarrassed to say those words out loud, but they were the truth. I'm not proud of what I was thinking way back then, but if I'm to be completely honest with myself there's no way around it.

"I was angry with God. Really angry," I confessed as I kicked some loose gravely towards the tree line. "I couldn't understand why he was putting me through that. Why he gave me a disease that nobody else that I knew even heard of before. He took my life and turned it upside down, and it really got to me. What was the worse though, was that God was putting my family through this as well. We did everything the right way. We went to church. We prayed as a family, at meals, and before going to bed. We were God fearing Christians, and He still felt the need to almost rip our family apart with this disease." At some point I had balled my fists up so tightly my knuckles were turning white. I shook my hands out and wiggle my fingers, trying to get the blood flowing back to them as I took a deep breath. I guess looking back at what we went through, I still got upset at God.

"I didn't see that coming." Lou looked surprised with my angry confession.

"Well, if you didn't see that coming, then you'll never be able to guess what happened next."

"You've got my attention. So what happened next?"

"I was in a dark place. A really dark place. Angry with God. Angry with myself, and feeling like I was a burden on my entire family. Then God did something for me. Something happened that changed my

15

direction in life. God plucked me off of my dark path and showed me a much brighter one."

"How did He do that? He didn't cure your epilepsy, right? What huge event happened that put you back on the right path?" Lou asked, seemingly riveted with my every word. He took a small step back, not as to draw away, but just to get a better, full view of my face.

I took a deep breath, but my voice still quivered a bit as I said, "He gave me what I still say is the greatest day of my life."

"Greatest day? Why? What happened to you that day?" I could tell he was on edge, trying to figure it out before I said anything else. "So, come on, spill it … what happened to you?"

I am not sure how far we had hiked to this point, but we went almost the entire way walking side by side. As Lou asked his last question, he quickly spun in front of me, stopping me dead in my tracks.

I took a step closer to him and looked him square in the eye. My smile got a little wider as I tried to gage his reactions.

"So what happened to me?" I repeated.

"I died."

PART 3...

I've seen that look before. Somewhat dazed, somewhat intrigued, a lot confused.

"Excuse me? Did you, ummm, did you say that you died?" he stammered.

"Yeah, you heard me right."

"Ok, so you died. Didn't see that one coming."

The shock on his face was expected. I was a little taken aback, however, when he strode over to a small bench by the water and sat down.

"So my little revelation makes you tired of walking around? Need to take a break?" I said, joking with him.

"Nah" Lou said clearing his throat a little, trying to keep his composure, "I feel just fine. Figured I might as well get comfortable, because there's no way you're dropping a knowledge nugget like that and not telling me the whole story."

"It's not really a short story. Everything I just explained to you basically led up to the intense journey that I got to go on."

"I'm perfectly good with that," he said as he sat back and took a quick drink from his bottled water.

"This bench is comfortable and I have no plans the rest of the day. So let's hear it."

"Fine, you asked for it."

I closed my eyes, and the light breeze took me back. Took me back to that day in August when my story started.

"That day was a perfect summer's day." I began. "Bright sun, no clouds, no place that we had to be, it just didn't get any better for a thirteen year old in the summer! A perfect day for a summer swim ...."

* * *

"Our parents put up a pool at the end of our property, so any hot day turned into a day at the pool. We normally had to work every weekend at my parent's business, but that one special weekend we had off, so we were looking forward to doing nothing but jumping in the pool. Of course, they put my older sister in charge of everything, and my mom made sure I knew without a doubt who was the boss for the day. And not only that, but to make sure I helped Angie by playing with my younger sister and keeping her happy."

"The way you are with your sister being your boss? I bet that went over well." Lou interrupted with that sly grin again.

"Oh yeah, you bet. I didn't like it one bit that Angie had the authority to tell us what to do. But I figured let's just get out to the pool and have some fun. She could be in charge all she wants, as long as I get to swim. I was a fish back then, still am really.

You put me in the water and you'll have to fight to get me out."

"So anyway, my younger cousin, Elisabeth, came over to play as well, and that really made the day great for me. I might have felt invisible to my own two sisters, but my cousin seemed to always look up to me. It was a much needed boost to the ego to have somebody interested in me. That always made me feel special. So, we were out the door and on our way to the pool before our parent's car was even out of the driveway. My mom yelled at me to be careful and to remember that my sister and cousin were still too young to be alone and that they couldn't swim."

"Well, I knew that Anita and Elisabeth couldn't swim, so I was the big dog in the pool. I would try to show them how easy it was to go underwater, how free it felt to swim around, but they were just too young and didn't quite pick it up. No biggie though, just trying to teach them made me feel more grown up. Of course, Anita kept giving me a hard time, but Elisabeth was watching me intently the entire time. Finally, when it was obvious neither of them were going to learn to swim that afternoon, I figured it was my chance to start showing off a little bit. I started doing flips under the water; trying to see how many rotations I could make before coming up for breath. Elisabeth would count each turn I would make. After a few minutes of that, I would sit at the bottom of the pool while Elisabeth once again counted to see how long I could hold my breath. I loved this! Angie and Anita never wanted to play these games with me!"

"If you guys had a pool and you were such a fish, you had to have messed around in the pool with your sisters. Were you a sad little girl because nobody would play with you?" We both laughed at the sarcastic baby voice he used.

"Well my younger sister couldn't swim, and my older sister was more interested in lying out and getting that golden summer tan. So, basically, I was on my own whenever we all would head out to the pool." I explained.

"With my cousin there, I at least had somebody that would *watch* me show off. After being in the pool for just a little while, Angie made us get out and go inside. She said it was to make sure that we got something to eat for lunch, but I think it was more likely that she wanted to call her friends. After all, she was 16 and always on the phone with somebody."

"Oh yeah, the good old days before cell phones, right? You were tethered to the wall, and could only move as far away as the phone cord would allow. Kids nowadays don't know how good they really have it!" Lou chimed in.

"Definitely, no doubt!" I agreed. "You have no idea how different this whole day would have turned out if we had cell phones back then."

"Ahhh, foreshadowing. Love it. So what happened? You guys stay inside for awhile? Your sister makes you sit around and watch her talk on the phone?" He joked.

"Not at first, but you're pretty close. We went back outside for a little bit after we ate lunch, but after being in the pool again for just a short time before

Angie said we were done outside for the day and that we were going to head back into the house."

"Wow, bet you loved that. Not only bossing you around, but making you get out of the pool. Two things that sound, from what I've been hearing, are very high on your list of things that you just *love!*"

"Yeah, well not this time. This time I decided I was done being bossed around. It was time I stood and became my own person. I was tired of being the stereotypical 'forgotten middle child,' and for once I was going to fight back. I wasn't going to let her boss me around. I wasn't going to be a good girl and do exactly what I was told. I was going to do what I wanted. And what I wanted was to stay in the pool."

"A teenage angst-ridden power struggle? What could possible go wrong with that?"

I wasn't quite sure if he was being serious with that question, or just joking around again.

"Since you put it that way, ALOT could go wrong. They kept saying that I was sick, and couldn't be by myself. That with my epilepsy, I had to be *'watched'* at all times. What happened if I got sick when I was in the water by myself? What happened if I had a seizure in the water?"

I could feel myself getting heated again as I was explaining this. They were hitting all my buttons. I felt different, and I knew I was different. I knew that I had some type of sickness and shouldn't be by myself. But I was also sick of being told that. Sick of being treated differently. Sick of not being allowed to be a normal kid. They didn't have to keep reminding me of all those facts. I felt it was time I became my own person and did whatever I wanted to do.

"My sisters got mad at me, and after a short yelling match with Angie, she told me that they were both going inside and I could stay in the pool if I wanted. My cousin could stay out there, but she wasn't allowed in the pool with me, and, last but not least, she said that my mom would definitely be hearing about how I wouldn't listen and fought with her!"

"Ooooh, you're in trouuubblle!!" he was laughing once again.

"Nah, never got that far. Once my sisters were back in the house, I felt I had won the battle. I might end up losing the war, but at least this one battle I came out victorious."

"So, my cousin and I were alone at the pool now, and I completely forgot about the fight with my sisters and went back to having fun. At least for a short time. I was in the middle of doing continuous flips under water again, you know, acting like a big-wig to my cousin, and that's when things went south."

"I was still underwater, and I remember having the strangest feeling. I felt tired. Just really tired. And my head felt a little fuzzy. I know I thought to myself that maybe I was swimming too soon after eating and that maybe I should get out for a while."

"Ah, that old wive's tale about waiting 30 minutes after eating. I didn't think that was a real thing," Lou said

"I didn't think it was either, and I didn't think I was feeling this tired because I had just eaten a sandwich for lunch. Well, my eyes felt heavy and my head was starting to tingle. I figured I'd just get out and lay by the pool for a bit until it passed. Then the next thing I knew, I am standing in the kitchen next to Angie."

"Wait a minute—aren't you still in the pool playing around? What do you mean you're standing next to your sister? I don't get it." I could tell he was utterly perplexed by my last statement.

"Just wait, it gets better. And by better I mean I'm sure you'll be really confused here in a second. So, not exactly sure how I got there, but I was standing by my sister listening to her talk on the phone to her friend. I called her name, to ask her what was going on, but she just ignored me. Didn't even look my direction. I know that she'd ignored me in the past, but something about this just seemed different. A little off. I was starting to get really confused, so I thought maybe Anita would know what was going on and how I'd gotten into the house."

"The instant I had that though, I was standing in the living room next to Anita. She was lying on the couch watching TV, and I couldn't explain it, but I somehow made it from the kitchen to the living room without remembering even moving."

"Were you having one of those seizures that just make you lose time? You know, not the big ones where you fall down and actually convulse, but just the ones where you stare off and don't realize what's going on around you?" he asked, looking as confused as I expected him to be.

"Yeah, that would have made sense to me too, but that wasn't it. I was standing next to Anita, trying to talk to her and she was ignoring me too. She should have at least acknowledged that I was there, you know? Told me to leave her alone or go back outside, something. But all I got was silence. It was like neither of them even saw me there."

"Then out of the blue I realized that my cousin was still outside by the pool, or at least that was the last place I had seen her. Then the same thing happened again. I thought to myself *"oh no, Elisabeth!"* and within a blink of an eye I was standing right in front of her. Looking right at her, again, with absolutely no recollection of how I got outside and all the way to the pool."

"I think I'm starting to see a little trend here. So basically, you have no idea how it was happening, but you ended up near each of them without remembering moving, walking, or anything like that. Does that sound about right?"

I could see the wheels turning in his head as he was asking me this. He was smart, and I could tell he was searching for that one reasonable explanation as to what was going on. He was grasping for it, and he thought he was close, but he quite wasn't there.

"Yeah, but I finally realized how I was able to move around so quickly. Well, I say move around, but I guess that's a relative way of putting it. You see, I realized that as soon as I thought of one of my sisters or cousin's name, I was immediately right there by them. And what made that even more compelling was that each time I ended up in a new place, there was a sound. Like a strong breeze … a *'whooosh'* type of noise."

I've told this story—I don't know how many times—but hearing it out loud actually made me realize just how crazy it really did sound. I'm not quite sure how I would react if somebody was telling this to me. Since I lived it and was there for all of this, it made complete sense to me. The hard part now was finding the right way of explaining it to somebody, so they could truly understand what was happening.

"I know it sounds crazy, but that's exactly how it worked. Anita's name popped in my head, and *WHOOOSH* ... I was standing right beside her. Angie's name, *WHOOOSH* ...and I was looking right at her talking on the 'phone and listening to the radio. Elisabeth's name? '*WHOOOSH*' and I was back outside at the pool with her. It felt like I was transported instantly, and I was actually with all three of them at the exact same moment in time."

"So is that *whooosh* sound is something that you get with a seizure? Just a noise you hear in your brain when it starts to misfire?"

"Sounds logical, but no. When I had a seizure, I would feel a tingling sensation in my head, but never heard anything like that. This was something completely different. This was a sensation that I've never felt or seen before. But my next "*WHOOOSH*", if I can put it that way, really let me know what was going on."

"So this *whooosh* is something brand new to you, and obviously you have no idea what it is, right? So you figured it out after just a few of them?"

"Pretty much but I'll get to that. So I was standing next to Angie, and just had a really strong feeling that

25

she needed to go out to the pool. I yelled for her to go outside, but she just kept talking on the phone. I didn't know why I had that feeling yet, but I just knew that she had to get out there as fast as possible. I remember thinking that if Angie couldn't hear me, then maybe Anita will now. So guess what happened once I thought that?"

"Yep, standing right next to her, right?" He finally answered one of my questions correctly.

"That's right. Looking right into Anita's face I yelled, well … I thought I yelled … to get up and get Angie. That they both needed to go outside right away. I didn't know if it was something subliminal or what, but she finally got up and yelled to Angie that she was heading back out to the pool. Angie told her to not go in the water, and she would be out in a bit after she got off the phone."

"So she heard you, right?"

"Still not sure about that, but at least she was heading outside to check on Elisabeth, and that's when the next 'Whooosh' happened and showed me what was really going on."

"Well you already told me that you died, so I am guessing it's around this time that it happened? Wow, that just feels weird saying it out loud. You died." His voice softened to a whisper as he talked.

"As soon as I whooooshed again and was outside with Elisabeth, I realized I wasn't standing next to her on the deck. She was sitting on the edge of the pool, just blankly staring into the water, and I was right in front of her. Right in front of her and right on top of the water. I looked down and saw that I was hovering about two feet over the water. I knew that something had happened to me in the pool, and this just confirmed my thoughts. Because not only did it appear I was sleeping under water on the bottom of the pool, I could also now see what Elisabeth was staring at in the water. It was me. I could see myself lying at the bottom of the pool. I was curled up in the fetal position and was completely motionless. I was only a few feet from the ladder, so it looked as if I had been heading to get out, but something had happened and I never made it. Not sure if I hit my head on the bottom of the pool or actually had a seizure while I was doing the flips.Either way, I ended up lying at the bottom."

"Whoa, crazy. So you could actually see yourself just lying there? Could you, like, see from underwater where you actually were too? You know what I mean?"

"Nah, I wasn't in my body at that time. I know it's hard to understand, but that form under the water wasn't really me. Well, I mean it was my body, but my 'spirit' wasn't under the water. It was already gone. Already out of my body and I guess you could say hanging out with my sisters and cousin."

"Wow, fascinating. So you were you with all three of them, and at the bottom of the pool at the same time. That can really mess with your mind." He was finally starting to grasp the full extent of what was going on now.

"Actually if you take a step back and really think about it, this wouldn't so much mess with your mind as expand it. You see, I realized that in the place where I was, my spiritual self that is, time, as we know it, didn't exist. In our linear way of thinking about time, there was no way I could possibly be in three places at the exact same instance. But in whatever realm or dimension I was now in, time didn't exist. I could be anyplace, all places, wherever I wanted at the exact same moment."

"So could you see your face? I mean, not sure what even to ask ... but what were you thinking when you saw yourself floating in the pool?"

"First off, I wasn't floating. I wasn't doing the 'dead man's float' that you think of or see in the movies. It looked like I just sank to the bottom. I was literally lying on the bottom with my eyes closed. Guess it just looked like I was sleeping," I said with a shrug. "Now this is where the story gets even *more interesting.*"

"Really? You've already set a pretty high bar. So, what happened when you were looking at yourself in the pool?" He looked like he was once again trying to figure out where the story went before I told him.

"It wasn't really me that caught my attention in the pool—it was what was with me down there. The water was really clear, so I could easily see the position my body was in, and it was even easier to see because there was some sort of glow around me. At first I thought maybe it was the sun, and it was just a direct beam or something concentrating the light onto me. Or maybe it was just my mind playing tricks on my eyes. But the closer I looked, the more I could see something was a really there. And it wasn't the sun. I didn't think it was coming *from* me, but it was a golden light *surrounding* me. Like I was safe within a golden cocoon." my voice trembled slightly as I tried explaining.

"Safe from what? You already drowned and weren't breathing on the bottom of the pool. Even if there was something there to 'protect' you, wouldn't you say that it was a little too late?"

"Oh no, whatever was causing that glow really was protecting me. You see, I wasn't alone in the pool. There were ... I don't know ... things in there with me." I knew the words I wanted to use to describe the things in the pool, but I wasn't sure if Lou was ready to hear them.

"Things?" he asked. "Did they look like animals or something?"

"Nope, not animals. They were extremely shiny and jet black. They didn't have any definitive shape about them, and they moved around the bottom of the pool effortlessly. Almost like oil slicks. I saw two or three of those things, and they were sliding along the bottom of the pool, circling my body, but always staying at least a couple feet away from me, just outside that golden glow that I told you about. They changed shapes as they kept going around and around, and every once in awhile, one would try to penetrate my protective golden halo. One end of the oily looking blob would form almost what looked like a mouth with jagged teeth, and for a second it looked like it was going to try to bite my body, or even swallow it whole. But once it touched the golden color, there was almost like a spark and the black creature would jump back. It was like it got shocked, and no matter how badly those things wanted to get to me, and believe me I saw them try over and over again while I was hovering above them, they couldn't get anywhere near me. I was protected from those things by that golden glow." I scanned his face, looking for some type of reaction.

He had a reaction, that's for sure. It really wasn't what I expected.

"You can say it," he said without flinching.

"Say what?" Now I was a little confused. Hadn't I already said enough?

"You can say what those black, oil patches in the pool with you were. We both know." He seemed to want to hear me say what he was thinking.

"Fine. Demons. My body was surrounded by demons, and they were doing anything they could to get to me."

We both sat there quietly for what seemed like an eternity. It was one thing to tell somebody that you died, but it was something else entirely to tell them that you then saw demons trying to get to your body. This was the part of the story that my grandmother kept telling me to keep to myself. People will either think you're crazy or be scared away because you 'see demons.' I heard that all the time.

Looking at Lou right now though, he didn't seem scared. And he didn't really seem to be looking at me like I am some crazy woman who sees things.

"I can't tell what you're thinking. Do you think I'm crazy or not?" I had to break the silence.

"Yeah, you very well could be crazy," he replied, "but not necessarily because of what you just told me. If there's a God and a devil, good and evil, then why wouldn't there be demons trying to do Satan's work? Good thing you had that protective glow, or whatever it was that you called it, keeping them away from you."

"You're not kidding. I've always heard about demons, but I do believe that this was the first time I ever saw one live and in the flesh! Or whatever it is that they have."

"So, how long were you under the water? No way your cousin would be able to get you out of there by herself, right?"

"No, remember when I said Anita might have heard me and started coming outside? She came all the way out to the pool, and once she got up next to Elisabeth, I heard her ask how long I'd been under the water. My cousin didn't say a word, and she must have realized something was wrong and jumped into the water to try to pull me out."

"Could she even move you? She had to have been about the same size as your cousin.No way either of them could have done anything."

"She tried. She didn't even know how to swim, but she still pulled at me with all her strength. I never budged though."

"Did those black demon-things do anything to your sister? Did she even realize that they were in there?"

"No, when she was pulling at my arms trying to get me above the water, she was inside that protective halo, so the black creatures were getting zapped and pushed away before they could get to her too."

"She realized that there was no way she was going to get me out of there," I continued, "so she climbed out and started running and yelling for Angie to come out and help. She was able to move me around enough and I finally floated up off the bottom of the pool. Now I really was doing the dead man's float. So, circle back around, and I am still with Angie trying to get her to hear me and come outside. She never did hear me, but she did look out the kitchen window at just the right time and saw Anita running and screaming for her. She hung up the phone right away and headed outside."

"Wow." Lou's eyes looked as if they'd pop out of his head and genuinely seemed concerned once again. "So how long did all this take? Seems like you'd been under the water for a really long time at this point."

"Not really. It actually only had been a few minutes. I guess that's still a long time to be under water and not breathing, but it wasn't an extremely long period of time at this point. Anyway, Angie jumped into the water just like Anita did and tried to get me out, but I was literally dead weight and she couldn't lift my body. My head was above water now, but since I wasn't breathing anyway, it didn't matter too much. She tried giving me mouth-to-mouth while we were both still in the pool, but she'd never done it before and really had no idea what she was doing."

"Man, you must have been freaking out watching all this. Weren't you afraid that they couldn't do anything for you?" Lou asked, still with an awestruck look on his face.

"Nope. Actually, at this point I felt completely at peace. I had no feeling of dread or despair, I wasn't scared. I simply felt at ease throughout this whole scene. Kind of hard to figure out why I wasn't freaking out, but whatever '*dimension*' my spiritual being was in, I felt perfectly fine. I wanted to tell them all that everything was going to be okay, that I felt fine where I was at that moment, and they didn't have to be so scared."

"Maybe that golden glow around you was giving you that peaceful feeling," he said.

"Who knows, but I felt great. You know ... for being dead." That little quip lightened the mood slightly, and I could tell he appreciated my sense of humor on the whole incident, but he still had an uncertain look on his face.

"So how did you finally get out of the water? Nobody that was with you was strong enough to lift you at all, so there's no way they were getting you out on their own, right?" The concerned look still hadn't left his face.

"First of all, you don't have to look so worried." I smiled at him reassuringly. "It was a crazy day, but as you can see I made it through just fine."

"Next," I continued without missing a beat, "Angie yelled for Anita to run to our neighbor's house and have them call an ambulance. Anita had nearly made it to my best friend Shane's house when Angie's pleas for help were answered. Gary lived in the house behind us, and must have been doing some yard work. He apparently heard Angie's screams and was over the fence and into the pool in a matter of seconds. Obviously he was much bigger and stronger than my sisters, so he had no problem lifting my body out of the pool and gently placing me on the deck."

"Lucky he was around. Odds are you wouldn't be here right now if he wasn't home that day, right?"

"Yep, he pulled me out of the water and saw I wasn't breathing. He asked if anybody had called an ambulance yet, and Angie said Anita was going to get our other neighbors to call. We could see her already coming back with my friend Shans mom, so they both knew that an ambulance was on its way. Gary told Angie that she needs to go to the house and call my parents, that I'll be okay and that he'll take care of me until the paramedics showed up and ..."

"With everything going on and how terrified your sisters seemed to be, I completely forgot that your parents still had no idea what had been going on." Lou blurted out. "Sorry," he said, "didn't mean to cut you off like. I just can't even comprehend how you would even tell your parents that something like that happened to a family member."

"I thought the same thing. Between trying to get used to that weird '*whooshing*' feeling and trying to get my sisters to realize what was going on, I didn't think of my parents until Gary mentioned them. And, of course, once I heard him say that, I couldn't stop thinking about them, and before I knew it, I was standing in my parents' office, watching him talk on the phone."

"Another *whoosh* moment I take it?" he asked.

"You know it. So, while Angie was heading back to our house and our kitchen phone to call my parents at work, I was immediately transported to the back office at my parents work. My dad was on the phone, not with Angie, but with somebody else. Not sure who. My mom was just off to my left, putting some paperwork away in the filing cabinet. For the first time since this whole thing started, a twinge of anguish started to creep up on me. Seeing my parents, going about the day like every other day they spend at work, having no idea what had been going on back home …." I trailed off.

For awhile when I was younger I hated the fact that my parents worked so much. Every single weekend they would be 'at the office.' Most weekends we had to go with them and help, rarely getting a Saturday off. It felt like the only thing we ever did together as a family was work. They had always been self-employed, always owned their own business, but I could never understand why they had to work so many hours. If they were the bosses, couldn't they stay home whenever they wanted? Couldn't they find somebody else to run the business for a weekend so they could be home with us playing in the pool?

Looking back now, I can see why they had worked so hard. Why they'd sacrificed weekends with us in order to spend time at work. They wanted nothing but the best for us kids, and putting in long hours and earning as much money as possible was one way they figured they could do that. One way they could get us nice things that we'd enjoy.

Like the swimming pool.

The pool that was now the center of what had turned out to be one of the strangest and most pivotal days in our family's history.

"Standing there looking at them hard at work, my heart just broke. I knew once Angie called them and told them what was going on, they would just be devastated." I said ... "But my dad was on the phone, obviously not talking to Angie yet because he was still in a good mood. I tried yelling for him to hang up, that Angie would be trying to call .... but of course, he couldn't hear me."

"Couldn't he just click over when she called? Oh wait ... I forgot how old you are. No call waiting back then, huh?" Lou said.

"Ha ha, yeah, back in the good ole days you could only be on one call at a time. Remember what a busy signal sounded like? I knew Angie would hear nothing but that if he wouldn't hang up the phone in the next few seconds."

"Ok, let me just get this straight one more time before you keep going. Seems to be a lot happening right about now and I wanna make sure I got it." he said. "So at this very moment, you are in your parents' office, trying to get your dad to hang up the phone."

"Yep, looking right at him."

"And you're standing next to Angie at your house, watching her dial the phone to call your parents."

"Right again."

"While you're also in the yard with Anita and our neighbor."

"Uh-huh, right again."

"While you hover a foot over the water in your pool ..."

"Wow, you're good."

"All while you're looking down at your actual *body* that's getting CPR performed on it by your other neighbor, Gary. Does that sound about right?"

PART 3…

"You summed it up pretty nicely. You're following along just fine." I commended him with a bright smile.

"So anyway, there I am yelling at my dad to hang up the phone, or he'd miss Angie's call. Then all of a sudden, he got a really strange look on his face and pulled the phone's handset away from his ear and looks at it. He said *'Angie, is that you?'*"

"But he never hung up the phone! How did her call get through?

"Even to this day, we still have no idea how her call got through. All I know is that my dad said one second he was talking to a vendor about work stuff, then all of a sudden the line kind of went dead and then he heard Angie's voice."

'Dad…it's Tina!' That's all Angie said, and I saw my dad jump up from his chair, slam the phone down and grab his car keys all in one motion. My mom was still off to my right putting stuff into a file cabinet. She had a confused-scared look on her face when she saw my dad jump to his feet. He just repeated what Angie said to him, *'It's Tina,'* and my mom dropped all of the paperwork and files she had been holding and raced behind him out the door."

"So it's come full circle now, everyone knows what happened and are either there with you by the pool or on their way there, right?" He finally got up and stretched his legs out. I guess we'd been sitting there longer than I realized.

"Yeah, you might want to stretch and get the blood flowing, the next part of this journey I'm telling ya is a doozy."

"Oh, so it gets even better?" Lou said as he sat back down on the bench. He leaned back and crossed his outstretched legs. "Don't get me wrong, it's been a crazy good story up to this point, but you keep talking about this *journey*. I can't wait to see what this journey to the best day of your life is all about!"

"It's definitely a journey you won't forget. Just sit back and enjoy the ride and please hold your questions until the end."

I leaned back slightly and closed my eyes, and I was immediately back by the pool. The feel in the air, the smells, the sun on my face. I was there again. I could see everybody, my sisters, my parents, Gary, my body. It was all still so real and fresh in my mind, every aspect of that day seemed like it had just happened yesterday.

"Now lets' see, where was I ..."

* * *

Looking down from my vantage point above the pool, I could see Gary feverishly giving me CPR. I wasn't breathing when he pulled me out of the water, and he was doing everything he could to breathe life back into my lungs. When Gary would move to the chest compressions, I could see my face. My skin was a purplish-white hue, and my lips were a pale shade of blue due to the lack of oxygen to my brain. My eyes were still open, but I could see a puss slowly oozing out of the corners. Off to my right, still standing in the yard were my sisters and cousin, huddling with Ms. Tadis. They all looked scared to death. That same feeling of heartache I had felt when I was with my parents overcame me.

Looking at the grief on my older sister's face just tore me up. I wanted to yell down to her that I was okay. That I loved her and that nothing that happened was her fault. It was my fault for fighting with her. For not listening and trying to be a grown-up when I really wasn't ready yet. I wanted to tell her that I wasn't in pain, or scared, and I had the most incredible peaceful feeling. I wanted so badly for them to know exactly how great I felt, but there was absolutely no way for them to hear me.

I heard a siren, slightly behind me, and when I glanced over my shoulder I could see the paramedics pulling a stretcher out of an ambulance that was parked in our yard. They were heading towards the pool where Gary had me breathing again, but just barely.

As they reached my body, one of the paramedics broke off to talk to my sisters. They needed to know if I had any medical conditions that they should know about, and if I was taking any medications. She was already so obviously flustered with everything that was going on, she kept stammering and stuttering as she tried to answer him. She then stopped, closed her eyes took a deep breath, and blurted out all the medications I was taking and that I had epilepsy. I wanted to reach down and hug her, tell her that I was proud of her and thank her for everything.

I looked back to the pool area, and the paramedics were putting my body onto the stretcher and telling Gary he did a great job. Thanks to him, I was breathing again, so I at least had a fighting chance. As soon as they strapped me down and started wheeling me towards the ambulance, my parent's car came flying into the back yard. I could see my mom jump out of the car before it even came to a stop, screaming for her baby girl. She hit the ground running, but slammed directly into a tree root that she must not have seen. I could hear her knee bang into the strong piece of wood, but she jumped right back up without flinching and met the paramedics just a few feet from the ambulance. She cried out again when she saw my blue coloring and heard my labored breathing. I was right beside her at this point, and wanted to put my arms around her tightly and tell her that I was just fine. I wanted her not to worry, and I wanted to let her know everything was going to be just fine.

She was running alongside the stretcher as they wheeled me to the back of the ambulance. The EMT was telling her that she would have to get back in her car and follow them to the hospital. I chuckled when I heard him say that.My mom might be small but she's definitely no push over. She's stubborn and mighty, and if she really wants something, like being with her daughter who was being rushed to the hospital—nothing was going to stop her. I think the EMT realized he had no choice in the matter, and relented to let her stay with me the entire time.

I was so intent on watching my parents, that I hardly noticed that my perspective of this whole scene was starting to change slightly.

I was no longer hovering somewhat above them. The closer my actual body seemed to get to the ambulance, the more I felt I was moving slightly higher.

I slowly looked around, and I could see I was now about ten feet above everybody else. From this vantage point I could actually see our entire property. And I noticed a strange glow coming from the horizon.

It was a golden glow. Once I saw it, I immediately recognized it as the same type of glow that was around my body in the swimming pool. It was that brilliant golden hue that was keeping those black oily blobs away from me, keeping me safe.

And as I watched them load my body into the waiting ambulance, I once again saw this golden glow.

Only this time it wasn't merely around my body or even around my spirit as I floated above my family.

It was surrounding the entire property.

Nobody else saw it, but it was a magnificent sight. As I stared into that protective light, I tried to make out what was creating the light.

The closer I looked, the more I realized I could see one, then two people standing at the edge of our property, directly inside the light. At first I thought they were more neighbors coming to see what was going on in our backyard.

Then I saw a few more people on the other side of the pool towards the back of the yard. People I didn't recognize—but the closer I looked I realized these weren't curious onlookers.

In fact, they weren't normal people, but were actually the beings that were creating the light.

One looked at me and smiled, and I knew that instantly what, or better yet, who I was looking at.

Angels.

Dozens upon dozens of them, holding hands and encircling our entire property. They weren't *'standing'* in a circle like I first thought, but they were actually hovering right above the ground. It looked like each one was about two feet above the earth, just sort of suspended there. Some had wings, some didn't, but they were all somehow levitating off of the ground. They each emitted their own golden glow, and when they joined hands with the others in the circle they created a halo that completely surrounded everyone within our property. There were males and females throughout the circle. Well, I wasn't sure if Angels really had a gender, but for what I could comprehend in my mind, I could see both men and women angels.

It was beautiful. This must not only have been what was protecting me, but what was also giving me the peaceful feeling that I'd had the entire day.

Had they been there this entire time? I would think that dozens of dazzling angels surrounding our entire house would be a little hard to miss, so why was I just now seeing them?

Maybe being up a little higher in the air, made it easier.

Or maybe I couldn't see them until I was ready. But ready for what?

As I looked at the scene unfolding below me, scanning the yard and seeing dozens of God's Warriors smiling at me, I started to realize that I was ready.

I always felt that we were surrounded by angels, and even if we couldn't see them, they were always around to watch over us. Now, when it felt like I needed them most, they revealed themselves to me.

I was so transfixed by the glory of the angels that I almost didn't noticed I was slowly starting to move again. This time there was no *'whooshing'* or quick movements, but I was slowly drifting upwards. I could see them closing the ambulance door with my body and mom inside while the rest of my family were quickly heading to the car to follow them to the hospital.

I continued to gently move upwards, although still not taking my eyes off of the scene that was wrapping up below me. Higher and higher, the picture of what could possibly be my last day on Earth was becoming more and more distant.

It now felt that I was being gently pulled upward, and I was starting to move faster and faster.

The final light from my previous life seems so far from me now. It looked slightly like a faint light coming through a small keyhole. In a blink of an eye, the final spark of light that I could still make out was extinguished, and I was now in utter darkness.

I was completely engulfed in blackness, not a speck of light no matter which direction I turned my head. The blackness was so dense—it made my eyes ache.

There was nobody around. I couldn't see anyone else within this darkness. However, for some reason I knew that I wasn't alone. I could feel two beings with me. One on either side, helping to guide me through the blackness. I didn't believe they were actually touching me, but I sensed their presence. It gave me the same peaceful feeling that I'd had on Earth only seconds earlier.

I was completely at ease; following the direction that my Guardian Angels were leading me without any worries.

Slowly a few dim lights started popping up around me. I was picking up so much speed that the lights where whizzing by me now, looking like shooting stars flying right past me. I was thinking to myself that this must be what it's like when you hit warp speed when flying through space. Yeah, can you tell that I loved Star Wars and Star Trek?

Anyway, more and more lights were spiraling around me now, exploding with multiple colors. I couldn't really tell how close they actually came to me, but they looked like small galaxies. Hundreds of them, coming at me from all directions.

Stunningly beautiful, I wanted to see them all, but there were simply too many of them. Then straight ahead of me, a pinpoint of light on the horizon appeared. It was so tiny and looked so far away, but at the speed I was moving, I thought I could probably get to it in no time.

As I continued moving forward, the pin point of light slowly began to grow. The darkness surrounding me was being filled by the streaking, spiral lights, but I couldn't take my eyes off of that spark. That growing beacon of light.

I knew where I was and where I was heading. And I knew exactly what I was looking at. Everyone in my life told me this was right.

There really is a light at the end of the tunnel.

* * *

"Whoa …" Lou finally said, "so, you were actually going through a tunnel? The one that you always hear about when you finally die? So, that's really a thing?"

"Oh it's definitely really a thing. One of the most incredible sights you could ever hope to see. Although it completely pales in comparison to where that little worm hole of a tunnel took me."

Many people have asked me about this journey, but I've never gone into this much detail. Normally when people hear the *'I died when I was thirteen'* phrase, I just give them the quick and condensed version. It seems like sometimes people are really interested in the fact that they met someone who had a near death experience, but they seem to shy away or close up once they hear the spirituality of the entire experience. Dying and coming back, yeah that's pretty cool and people like to hear that, but make it too religious of a story and they seem to wither away a little.

Lou seemed a little different. He didn't even flinch when I mentioned the angels. He looked like he was completely into the fact that I was going through the tunnel, and he seemed genuinely interested in what laid ahead once I reached the light.

I think he understood the fact that you can't really have a story like this one without a spiritual aspect to it. If that's the case, then he'd really get a kick out of what I was about to tell him next.

"Pales in comparison, huh. I'm guessing it wasn't flames and pitchforks that you saw next, was it?"

"Yeah, you joke about that, but I've heard people with similar stories heading in the wrong direction, if you know what I mean. No pitchforks or flames on this journey though, sorry to disappoint!"

"Scary thought, but no disappointment here," he said. "I have a feeling I know what's in the light, sort of ...."

"Yeah, or so you think. Let's get back to the tunnel first, shall we?"

* * *

As I continued to speed towards the ever-growing light, I looked around once more, and although I couldn't see anyone else in the darkness, I knew I wasn't alone. I was no longer being pulled backwards. I had turned over and was now facing forward heading to that ever growing pinpoint of a light. Knowing that I was riding the wings of my angels gave me such a peaceful and safe feeling.

The anticipation of what was next was almost unbearable! Anytime now, I'd have to be almost to the end of the tunnel. Gotta be soon! The small spark of light had grown immensely, and I could actually feel the light now. I It was so warm! So inviting! So much love! I'd never felt so at ease, and so peaceful than I did at that moment.

I felt I must be close now...

As I entered the light, I could faintly make out some shapes ahead of me. Or I guess you could say below me. It looked like I was heading right for somebody that was kneeling down inside the light. I could feel myself slowing down slightly, my entire body was tingling and I finally heard that familiar sound that I'd heard all day ...

WHOOOSH...

I found myself looking down at my hands folded in front of me, and I realized that the kneeling body I had seen was me. I knew exactly where I was now. I felt comforted, loved. Finally at ease. It felt right.

I was in Heaven.

I was home.

I looked down past my folded hands and saw that I was now dressed in a pure white robe. Crisp, perfectly white, no folds, no fuzz. I'd never had one like this before. I gazed down further and noticed I was kneeling on what looked like incredibly beautiful opal. I tilted my head slightly to get a better look, and the color changed. With every little movement of my head, I saw different colors swirling around on the ground below me. Magnificent blues, reds, golds, all moving around my bended knees.

It was mesmerizing.

I leaned down a little closer to get a better look, and I heard a small noise coming from something below me. Was that a humming sound? Almost sounded like music? But where was that coming from? As I concentrated on that rhythmic hum, I realized that it was coming from the ground. The colors that I was staring so intently at seemed to be giving off musical notes. I carried my gaze a little farther out and realized that the entire ground around me was made of this musical opal.

I glanced to my left and saw a small wall, about three feet high. It looked like it was made entirely of soft, smooth pearl. More magnificent colors; white, yellow, pink. Each one had their own magical hum to it, just like the opal that I was still kneeling upon. I looked over to my left and realized that the wall encircled me. It continued on to my right in a spherical shape and looked to wall off the small little courtyard that I was in right now.

I was completely alone within this little area. I could still sense my protectors near me, but there wasn't another soul in sight. I guess you could say that literally, there were no souls around.

Then I saw her. Well, at first I couldn't really tell what I was seeing, it was basically a blurred figure on the other side of the wall off to my right. I couldn't really make out who it was, but then slowly my focus on it, well, on her, started to sharpen.

She was my grandmother! Looking exactly as I had remembered her before she died years earlier. The dark circles under her eyes, body hunched over after a lifetime of hard work raising a family, she still appeared extremely tired. Although she looked beautiful to me, she didn't appear exactly as I had expected. I figured that if I saw any relatives up here in Heaven, and yes, I knew that was exactly where I was, all of their little aches and pains they had gotten during their lifetimes would be healed. She seemed happy, but she still appears to be in physical pain and anguish.

Just as I was thinking that, something amazing began to happen.

I was still staring at her, when, for some reason, her face began to change. Her whole body seemed to be transforming right before my eyes. She was slowly morphing into a whole new person. In the blink of an eye, she stood behind that amazing pearl wall looking like a beautiful thirty year old. Her hair was now jet black, her skin perfectly smooth, and her eyes a stunning blue. She was gorgeous! She looked completely different, but when she glanced over at me and I was looking into her magnificent eyes, I could still see my old grandmother. She was the same person I knew and loved on Earth, only now her body was no longer riddled with pain.

She was wearing the same type of crisp white robe that I had on, and she was now standing next to two older women and one older man. Not sure where they came from, they just seemed to appear there. Maybe they were there the whole time, and I just couldn't see them until I saw my grandmother. I don't know, but whatever it was, I could see them clearly now. They were all dressed in identical robes, and although I knew that I have never met these people before, I instantly knew who they were. It was my great grandmother and grandfather, standing by my great-great grandmother, all from my mom's side of the family. They too looked ragged with age, but just as with my other grandmother, they seemed to magically morph into the bodies of their youth. I never had a chance to meet these family members, but seeing the expressions on their face and the love in their eyes, I knew I was home amongst family.

I shifted my gaze over my left shoulder, and saw more family members. These were members of my father's family. The two young ladies I was looking at now were my great grandmothers. I had heard stories about them, living in the 'Old Country' of Greece. Although I never got to meet them, they were just as I had imagined. Young, beautiful, full of life.

Full of life? Here? I remember thinking that and making myself chuckle just a little. Can somebody really be full of life if they are not alive? I didn't know, but that was the feeling I got when I looked into their eyes. Full of life and full of love.

I looked back down at my folded hands, and a wave of humbleness washed over me. These hands that I was looking at—my hands—were my family's hands. They were still young, not yet marked by the trials and tribulations that you go through in life. My ancestors' hands showed the years of wear and tear, years of hard life that they had to endure in order to make me what I was today. Abusive husbands, hard labor working in fields, families torn apart by war and famine. I was simply a humble little girl in the presence of my strong and proud ancestors. I was here because of their sacrifices.

I could feel myself start to blush, and I immediately looked back down at the musical ground I was still kneeling upon. Embarrassed? Yeah, somewhat. But most of all I felt selfish. Selfish that I was usually only worried about how *my* life was going. How *hard* I always thought it was being the "forgotten middle child."

I slowly looked back up, and my ancestors were still just on the other side of the wall from me.

They were all smiling at me, no words were spoken, but they were no doubt reassuring me that they knew exactly who I was as well, and that I was loved. I didn't need to be ashamed or feel guilty for the hard times that they had gone through to help our family continue to grow.

I looked over in the direction they were heading and saw what looked like a white, marble gazebo. Well, it wasn't just a white gazebo. It had a glittering shine to it that made it appear to be constructed of gold and diamonds. Had that been there this whole time? I didn't notice it until now, but once I saw it, I realized everything around me revolved around this stunning piece of architecture. I wasn't really sure what I was looking at, but what I did know was that I couldn't take my eyes off of that spectacular white marble for some reason.

There were people heading towards the gazebo, but it didn't look like anybody ever went up into the center opening. It appeared empty, but it was a little hard to tell, since there was a bright golden light coming from somewhere in the center.

It wasn't a normal light coming out of the middle of the gazebo, but one I was sure that I'd seen before It was amazing, so golden, so warm and inviting, It quickly became obvious to me where I'd seen it before.

It was the same light I saw surrounding my body at the bottom of the pool, the same light that was emanating from the angels that had surrounded our property protecting me.

It was without a doubt the Light of God.

The light I was now looking at seemed to be directed straight at me, like it was a concentrated sunbeam shining solely onto my kneeling body.

I couldn't take my eyes off of the light, and slowly I could see someone standing in the middle of the glow. I hadn't seen him before, but there was no denying the fact that I could now see a silhouette directly in the middle of the gazebo.

I couldn't see a face, or really any features, but I could tell that it was a young man. He moved away from the center of the gazebo, and took a few steps towards the edge. As he did so, another figure appeared to the right of him. I still couldn't see any features, but I could sense this was an older person.

They moved in unison, when one took a step, the other took an identical step. Every movement was synchronized, like the two entities were sharing a mind. Sharing a soul.

It was at that point that I could sense another figure within the light, somewhere directly in the middle of the other two. This one I could see had a form, but it wasn't as clearly defined as the other two. It also moved in perfect harmony with the other two shapes within the light.

I could feel my jaw drop just a little. My mind finally comprehended exactly what I was seeing.

I was in the presence of God, and what I was gazing upon within that golden gazebo was the Holy Trinity.

It had to be. The scene unfolding in front of me made perfect sense at that point.

There was an older figure, the Father.

There was a younger figure, the Son.

And another figure that was ever present, but with no real form, the Holy Spirit.

My parents and grandparents always told me about this day, but I guess I never really thought much into it, that one day I really would be kneeling before God. My mind was racing, trying to figure out what I was supposed to do now.

I knew exactly who I was looking at, and I could feel that He knew as well. I looked over to where my relatives were standing, and they each had the same smile on their faces.

My gaze shifted from my relatives back to the gazebo, and the amount of love I felt was incredibly overwhelming. I'd never felt this much love. It was pouring into me and I was soaking it up like I was being baptized all over again. Only this time it wasn't Holy Water washing over me, it was literally God's love. I could feel the realization that every bit of knowledge that we so desperately want to learn while on Earth, we will know instantly here in Heaven. Anything you could possibly imagine. Why do we suffer? How was the universe made? What is the true meaning of life? All questions would be answered in time. God just hasn't revealed them to me yet.

There were people standing beyond where my family was. They were all walking on a golden path carrying what appeared to be a golden box. It looked like it was made of solid gold and had to have weighed a ton, but they were each holding one with apparently no effort whatsoever.

They joined the other people on this path, all carrying the same type of box heading towards God and His magnificent gazebo. They each had an unmistakable look of pure joy on their faces, and as they passed by the gazebo they looked up directly into God's light and bowed their heads. I followed their gaze and noticed when they looked into the gazebo. God slowly nodded back to each of them individually. They continued on the path around the gazebo to an open meadow with a slow moving river running through the far side. Just beyond the river, I could see multicolored mountain ranges stretching upward.

The colors I was seeing—I couldn't even begin to describe. All I could think was that they were heavenly colors, so bright and brilliant.

It seemed that everything around God worshipped Him, including the colors. Funny to think that colors could worship God. But the Bible does say that *the mountains and the hills before you shall break forth into singing, and all the trees of the field shall clap their hands.* (Isaiah 55:12), so why should the colors in Heaven be any different? The tones that the colors were giving off weren't simply musical notes. They were praises to God for just being.

Those musical colors reminded me how much I was loved. I knew I was created by God for God. I was His creation and He loved me no matter how angry I was with Him. I was His child and I always would be.

I looked back into God's light, trying desperately to see if I could actually make out a face, or even any type of facial features.

Somewhere in the back of my mind I could hear what sounded like an older man slightly chuckling. I looked around at all of the people moving past me, but I quickly realized what I was hearing was God Himself. He knew exactly what was in my mind and must have found it a little humorous that I wanted to know what He looked like. Wow, pretty cool ... I thought realizing He could *hear* me. Who knew that God had a sense of humor?

Then it hit me—if God could read my thoughts here, He *must* know about all of the bad thoughts I had about Him throughout the years. I was so angry with God when I found out I had epilepsy. I had thought it was so unfair. I couldn't understand why He gave me such a horrible illness and took away any hope I might have had for a normal childhood. I wasn't just mad at God, the thought actually crossed my mind that maybe there wasn't a God. Surely an "*ever loving*" God like we're taught in Sunday School would never set a kid on such a cruel path.

I never lost my faith, but it definitely wavered, and now here I was—humbled and kneeling before the same Holy Trinity that I once had questioned. I felt a twinge of embarrassment. A slight twinge of unworthiness.

The feeling of unworthiness I had felt when I had seen my long passed ancestors paled in comparison to the feeling washing over me at this moment.

I heard that slight chuckle once again, and the feeling instantly went away.

I quickly knew I was where I wanted to be. I knew I belonged here.

I knew I was home.

Once the chuckle in my head subsided, a new sound entered my head and that made my heart pound.

The voice of God.

"*Tina, go back. Your family and friends need you.*"
I felt the words deep in my soul.

Wait, what? I don't belong here? I might not have
fit in anyway back home, but I definitely felt like
I belonged here. I felt this was exactly where I was
meant to be.

Then the slight chuckle again, and the most
incredibly soothing voice I've ever heard once more
filled my head.

"*Go back and do my work. Your family and friends
need you. When your time comes, you will be here with
me. Until then, go back and do my work.*"

I looked around at all the other people walking
on their paths to the light behind Him.

'*Nah, I'm good*' I thought to myself knowing that
He would be able to hear it. '*I think I'll just stay here.*'

Why would I want to leave this place? A feeling
of pure love, pure joy, a feeling of complete content
and acceptance. Even though He told me to go back,
I still felt like I really did belong here. Then I heard
it one more time.

'*Tina, go back. Your family and friends need you.
When your time comes, you will be here with me. Until
then, go back and do my work.*'

I was looking directly into the light, and although
I still could not make out any features other than the
silhouettes, I could sense He was smiling at me. I was
no longer nervous, even though I just realized that I
basically told God no, and I didn't want to do what
He had asked. He created me, so He had to have
known just how stubborn I could be. It was a trait

I had in my Earthly body, and obviously was a trait that I brought with me here to Heaven.

'My family will be just fine,' I thought back to Him. *'Sure they'll miss me for a bit, but they'll move on. If I stay here, I'll no longer be a burden to them. No longer be the one that they always have to watch. They'll be able to live a normal life if I'm not there to hold them all back.'*

Once that thought came to me, I could see something happening from within the gazebo. The golden light remained the same, but the three figures slowly moved together into one being, one entity directly in the middle of the structure.

Maybe back in my Earthly body I would have had trouble trying to comprehend what I was seeing, but here in this moment I knew exactly what I was witnessing. The Holy Trinity had come together and formed one Holy Spirit. I just wasn't exactly sure why just yet.

This single entity had no real form to it, but was slowly drifting upwards. It went right through the roof of the gazebo and continued until it was just a few feet above the rounded dome of the gazebo. What looked like an arm extended out from one side and slowly motioned like it was trying to show something to me. The arm slowly moved upwards, and when it did, the sky behind it pulled back like a curtain revealing a movie theater style view of what was going on at this moment back with my family.

The scene I was watching wavered a little, and I was seeing my parents standing just outside of my hospital room. They were talking with my doctors, and while my dad just nodded while looking stoic, my mom was still sobbing. I could hear them tell my parents that I most likely would not come out of this coma. Odds were very slim that I would wake up, and if I did, I would never be the same. Since I had gone without oxygen for so long, I would be lucky to have the mentality of a small child for the rest of my life, however long or short that may be. In all honesty, they felt I wouldn't make it through that first night.

The doctors told my parents that for me to make a full recovery would take a miracle. Too much damage was done to my brain, and it swelled up so much that they might have to operate and drill a hole in my head to alleviate the pressure. They wanted to wait to perform that surgery though. They didn't feel I was strong enough to survive it since the only things keeping me alive at the moment were the machines breathing for me.

My parents were shocked, but they refused to believe them. They said they knew their little girl would wake up, and when she did, she would be the same old Tina as before. They had complete faith that God would deliver their child back to them, back where she was needed. The doctors understood. I'm sure they'd heard this from parents all the time in this situation, and they did their best to try to calm my parents and help them face what they believed to be an inevitable outcome. They wanted my parents to prepare themselves in the event that I didn't wake up, and to think about how long they would want to keep me on life support knowing it was basically a losing battle.

I glanced back down to the gazebo and the people that were still moving along their paths. I watched them each stop in front of the gazebo, then continue on their own paths without once even glancing up at the show in the sky that I'd been watching.

This movie must be for my eyes only.

I know this is really hard on them now, but in time it'll get easier, right? I thought to no one in particular, yet knowing exactly who would hear the question.

I wasn't sure what answer I was really expecting to get to that question, but He waved his hand again and the scene in the sky changed one more time.

My family was now back at our house. From the looks of it, I obviously didn't make it out of the hospital. Wow, instead of simply answering my question, God was showing me what my family's life would be like if I didn't go back.

My own little version of "It's a Wonderful Life," I guess.

I could see everyone was at home, but they were all in different parts of the house, doing their own things. I was not only watching each of them, but I could actually *feel* exactly what they were going through at that precise moment.

My sister, Angie, sat alone in her room listening to music. She had it turned up loud, but she obviously wasn't paying attention to it. There was a darkness to her that wasn't there before. The anguish and pain I felt coming from her was almost unbearable. There was an emptiness in her eyes, and I could feel how guilt ridden she was. She had been in charge. She was the adult. It was *her* fault that I had died. Her sister was gone because of her. She knew it, and she believed that the entire family felt the same way.

My parents tried not to blame her, but there was no doubt they harbored some resentment towards her. Every time they looked at Angie, no matter how hard they tried to fight it, they would be reminded of my lifeless body being pulled out of the swimming pool. The only way they figured they could stop that feeling would be to simply stay away from Angie. They were slowly drifting apart, not able to talk about anything without feeling the pain of losing a child.

Their relationships with my sisters were almost nonexistent. My poor younger sister was left alone, almost forgotten by my parents in their grief. My cousin no longer came to play with her. With the swimming pool being torn down, there were no more summer parties for her to look forward to. It looked like she sat alone most days, just blankly staring at the television or wandering around the house brushing her dolls' hair. Rarely showing any emotion, the carefree trouble maker that I knew her to be no longer seemed to be there.

Worst of all was the spiritual sense coming from my family, but mostly what was coming from my parents.

Or maybe I should say what I didn't feel coming from them.

There was nothing. No hope, no faith, no spirituality, no relationship whatsoever with God anymore.

They prayed for Him to return their little girl, and He didn't. Their prayers fell on deaf ears, and God ignored their pleas to keep their family whole. Why would they pray to and worship a God that would tear a family apart in this awful manner?

I just couldn't believe it. In the Greek culture, everything revolved around church and family. With me gone from their lives, it appears that those staples of normalcy no longer existed in their day to day life.

Could I have been wrong this whole time? Was I not really the invisible middle child? I knew my family loved me, but I always had that feeling in the back of my mind that if I were gone, things for them would move on like normal.

As if to answer my question, the sky opened up on the other side of the Holy Spirit, to reveal a new scene. It was my family at home again, however, this one was obviously much different from the somber one I had just viewed.

I had gone back, and I was with my family again. We were sitting together eating a Sunday dinner as one whole family. We were laughing, talking about the day, and I could literally feel the joy and love coming from every soul that was sitting around that dining room table.

I sensed that my relationship with my sisters was stronger than ever. The fact that we went through that ordeal together and I came out of it okay made us closer than I ever thought we could be. We would still have our fights, as all sisters do, but I knew without a shadow of a doubt that my sisters loved me with every fiber of their being. Something I was never quite sure of before I came here to Heaven, but this scene cleared all that up for me.

I watched as my parents looked at me with so much love and caring. I could feel myself getting a little teary eyed while the scene played out in front of me. They weren't just happy—they were at peace and full of love again.

On top of all of those personal feelings flowing from my family, there was one overarching sensation that I kept getting. There was another spirit with us the entire time, and once I realized what it was, I couldn't help but smile.

My family had welcomed God back into their lives once I had returned, and the strong sensation I was receiving was God's love embracing my family. Well, I know that God's love was always there surrounding them, but they were hugging Him back now. Their prayers were answered, and their faith and love for God grew even stronger after I was sent back into their lives.

Then the scene flashed once again, and evolved into little snippets of what was to come for me. Nothing more than a second or two each, but it was extremely easy to see the theme He wanted me to learn.

With each flash I would see a different person, a stranger to me that I had never seen before, but felt that I somehow would play an important role in their lives. I could feel God saying *"There are no accidental meetings. Coincidences do not exist,"* and I instantly knew he was going to put me on *their* paths for a reason. If I were truly destined to go back and do His work, these were just some of the people that I was meant to help. They each must be going through a difficult event or feeling some type of pain, but I could also feel that they felt somewhat better and more at ease after we would meet. I don't think that it was necessarily just meeting me that would help them out,--it was something more. I would be able to spread God's word to them and help them feel comfort at some point in their lives.

The selfish feeling I'd had when I saw my ancestors slowly came back. I was in paradise. I was happy and wanted to stay because of how great it made *me* feel. I didn't think of how it would make others feel or how it would impact their lives if I didn't return. I was only thinking about myself, and I was a little ashamed.

I couldn't do that to my family. I couldn't do that to all the others that I might be able to help later in life. My decision was made. But before I could even think it, I heard His voice once again.

'*Tina, go back. Your family and friends need you. When your time comes, you will be here with me. But until then, go back and do my work.*'

The scenes in the sky slowly faded away, and the Spirit that I saw in the sky gently descended and returned to the gazebo. Once again I could see the three figures that I originally had seen, and I could feel each of them smiling at me and filling my mind and body with so much love that it was almost overwhelming. The warmth within me went all the way to my core. I could just about feel my soul glowing and pulsating with His love.

I took one last look at my Creator, at the Holy Trinity that I prayed to every night, and I felt at peace with my decision. I knew I'd be back with Him when it was time, but until then I also knew He would be with me wherever my journey took me. I slowly took one more glance around over to where my ancestors once stood, but they were no longer there. They must have moved along on their path, already knowing that it wasn't right for me to stay with them yet.

All that was left was to agree with God, and ask Him to send me back.

I slowly bowed my head once again, looking down at folded hands and prayed that God returned me to my family.

I closed my eyes and smiled, knowing that shortly I would be back with my family, and then when my life's journey was over I'd be right back here in paradise.

My smile grew slightly wider as I heard that familiar sound welling up from somewhere deep within my soul.

"WHOOOSH..."

There were no tunnels this time, no slowly moving backwards or upwards. When I opened my eyes I was back on Earth, standing just outside a small hospital chapel.

My jaw dropped as I watched my parents sitting alone in the pews, praying to the God that I was just kneeling before. My father, pleading with Him to give back his little girl, that he needed his Tinkerbell. My mother, sobbing as she prayed that God would deliver me back from this awful accident. I could hear her say they needed me. They needed me so much more than God needs me right now.

I was standing in the doorway as they stood back up and started walking out, holding each other while my mom sobbed quietly into my father's arm. They walked right past me, and I wanted so badly to reach out and give them a hug, but I knew I couldn't.

Not yet, but soon.

As I watched them walk slowly back down the cold, sterile corridor towards my room, I noticed the lights seemed a little brighter than normal. Not so much as being overly bright, but they simply had a special glow to them.

This could only mean one thing—I wasn't alone on my journey back.

Standing right beside me was the source of the glowing hallway lights. It was a towering figure, a man who dwarfed everyone in the area, yet gave off such a comforting and soothing feeling I couldn't help but smile at him. He had sandy blond hair, and was wearing something similar to what an old Greek or Roman soldier would wear, complete with a shiny silver sword on his side. I knew he was there to help me on the final leg of this journey. My personal protector from day one—my very own guardian angel.

As we followed my parents down the hall, I couldn't help but think about what this protector must think of me. I knew I hadn't made things easy on him throughout my life up to this point, and we'd always joked about how hard of a job my guardian angel must have, but now that I was actually with him, I was starting to wonder if he'd gotten into any sort of trouble 'on the job' because of this whole drowning fiasco.

As if completely understanding what was racing through my mind, he gently placed his hand on my shoulder and gave me a knowing smile. There was no judgement or sign of contention whatsoever in the look he gave me. In fact, it was simply a look like a best friend would give. You know, the kind that says, "Don't worry—I got your back."

We stayed a few feet behind my parents as they continued down the hall toward my room. We watched from that vantage point as they stopped at the entry of a room on the right side of the hall. They didn't go in right away. Instead, they hesitated while looking to the left side of the room before slowly moving to a couple of chairs just inside the door to the right.

My mom sat down first, still sobbing and looking down, seemingly very reluctant to raise her head at all. My dad plopped down heavily on the chair next to her and just stared straight ahead with a pained look on his face that shook me to my core.

As I passed over the threshold into this small room, I followed his gaze off to my left to see what was causing so much pain and anguish in a man that I had never even seen shaken before in my life.

And for the first time, I could see myself as my family saw me right at that moment. Lying motion-less with wires and tubes running from my body to machines on both sides of the bed. I looked pretty good, I thought to myself, for being dead just a little bit ago.

I moved closer and looked at myself laying there, eyes closed and looking so peaceful. I knew this was just my 'human shell," a vessel to carry my soul through this Earthly journey. But to my grieving par-ents, this lifeless body that laid before me was their little girl. If they only knew the joy and wonder I had experienced while my body was in this vegetative state, they wouldn't be sad at all. They would have to be excited for me, happy that I had a chance to go someplace that very few people ever get to visit and return from.

But for right now, all they could see was one of their children dying right before their eyes. They had no idea what I'd experienced in the short time that my body had been laying in this hospital bed.

I turned and looked at my guardian angel, who was still standing right at the entrance of the room. Before I knew it, I was instantly sitting on the side of the bed, my legs dangling and swinging since they were too short to reach the floor.

My angel glided over toward me. His golden glow became brighter and seemingly filled the entire room with the brilliant light. It was so bright that I thought for sure my parents would *have* to see it. It flooded out of the room and into the hallway, filling up every space in the area.

He was directly in front of me now, and I could see clearly into his eyes, even as he was exuding that magnificent glow from seemingly every fiber of his being. I knew this part of my journey was over.

It was time to return to my Earthly body and begin fulfilling the promise that I made to God that I would come back and do his work.

I watched him carefully as he slowly raised his right hand, never losing eye contact with me. He seemed to say, *"Don't worry. You might not see me again for awhile, but just remember I'll be with you always."*

Before I could say or even think anything, he gently touched my forehead.

In a flash, the beautiful angel and his golden aura were gone. I was now staring at the dull fluorescent lights hanging above my hospital bed. I looked around, trying to get my bearings and figure out exactly what had just happened. Then I looked down toward the end of the bed and made eye contact with my parents. The realization finally hit me.

I was back.

My parents leapt to their feet and rushed to the side of my bed.

I was looking around the room wildly, trying to sit up. I wanted, no I *NEEDED* to tell my parents that I had just seen God!

My dad gently put his hand on my shoulder and told me to lie back down and try to relax. I could see my mom over his shoulder run to the door and yell for a doctor to come into my room. One must have heard her, because within seconds, she was right by my side with my father.

Things were a little blurry, but there was no mistaking who I was looking at now. My parents had a combination of shear fear mixed with excitement on their faces.

Before I knew it, there was a team of doctors and nurses rushing around my bed. There was only one look on their faces: pure shock.

Apparently, my parents were the only ones who truly believed I would eventually wake up, and when I didn't wake up that first night, the doctors never expected me to ever open my eyes again. If I had, I most likely wouldn't even recognize my parents. No surprise that there was nothing but shocked faces running around my room.

I could see everybody talking, but I really couldn't hear what they were saying. The only sound I could really hear was an annoying beep. Looking around the room, I realized what I was hearing were all the machines that I was hooked up to. Beeping and going crazy because I was awake and moving around.

I tried telling my parents that I was okay, that I was back from heaven and everything was going to be just fine now.

I was looking right at my mom, but no words were coming out. I felt what I first thought was a lump in my throat, but when I moved my hands up to my face, I realized I had a tube in my mouth. I don't know exactly how long my body was unconscious while I was on my little trip, but this tube must have been what kept me breathing. I'd never seen a breathing tube before, but I can tell you know what one feels like. And it's not good.

So that's why I can't talk. Pull it out now! I don't need it! Please! I have so much I need to say, but I can't say anything with all of these tubes in me!

I saw one of the nurses pushing a few buttons on the machine next to my bed, and that annoying beeping finally stopped. I could slowly start to actually hear what was going on in the room around me.

My parents told me that everything was going to be okay, just try and relax. The doctor's ran around yelling some medical stuff I didn't understand, and at the same time tried to get me to lay down flat on my back.

I knew I couldn't get out of the bed, but I frantically wanted to tell everybody that I was fine. I felt perfectly normal right now. I desperately wanted to tell them about the unbelievable journey I had just been on!

They wouldn't pull the tube out of my throat, and I couldn't figure out why. I laid my head back down on the pillow, but I continued to scan the room. First to my left, watching the nurses messing with the machines and my IVs, and then back to my right where my parents were huddled behind the doctors that were busy shining lights in my eyes, checking my vitals, and basically looking shocked that I was awake.

I could hear the doctor closest to me say to just lay back and let the machine continue to do all the breathing for me—don't fight it right now. I finally put my head down and watched as they put something into my IV that would help me "relax and get some rest."

Get some rest?? I screamed to myself. *I've been basically dead for three days! I don't need any more rest!*

I was still trying to talk and breathe on my own, and the burning in my throat from the breathing tube was starting to get a little worse. One of the doctors, the one that was shining his light into my eyes, had his hand on my forehead and continued telling me to relax, I would be fine and they were there to help.

My eyes were now burning too. Whatever they had put into my IV was starting to take effect, and I could feel myself becoming drowsy.

I looked past the doctors and my parents one more time, checking to see if anyone else was in the room with us.

There was nobody. The doorway was empty.

He was gone. My guardian angel, whatever his name might have been, was gone.

I looked over at my parents one more time and fell asleep.

* * *

I quickly sat up straight and looked around the park to see if anyone else was close enough to hear my little tale. There were plenty of people walking past us on the trail, but for all intents and purposes, we were alone.

I shifted slightly, starting to feel more than just a tad uncomfortable as I realized I'd been the only one talking for the last 15-20 minutes or so. It seemed like anytime I talked about my little swimming incident, I got transported back to that summer. It's so vivid in my mind. It truly feels as if I'm actually reliving the experience.

"So yeah, that's a little bit about who I am," I said finally turning my full attention back to Lou.

He was still staring at me, wide eyed and with his mouth slightly opened. That was exactly the expression that I was expecting to see.

"Any questions?" I said half jokingly.

"Well, um, yeah I think I could possibly come up with a few things. So you drowned."

"Yes."

"And you basically died."

"Yep."

"Went on a *journey* and now you're back here."

71

"Basically, that about sums it up. I guess I just could've said that and left everything else out."

"Nah, believe me. The way you said it was much better than that. Well, there's one obvious question ..."

"Shoot. I think I know what it is anyway."

"Ok, so how do you know it all really happened? It wasn't just a dream or something like that?"

"There it is, the number one asked question!" I knew it was coming and couldn't help but laugh each time I heard it.

"Not that I don't believe you—I really do. But that's such an incredible story. How do you explain that to other people you tell?"

"I understand, I get that a lot. After I woke up and was finally back home, I was able to tell my family things. Things that there was no way I would know unless I was actually *with* them while I was under the water and then hooked up on life support."

"Huh, interesting." He murmured.

"I told Angie exactly what song she was listening to while on the phone, Glenn Frey's *Boys of Summer,* in case you were wondering, and even who she was talking to. I let them know Anita was lounging on the couch watching one of those really cheesy afternoon soap operas. And the kicker, I could not only tell my parents who my dad was talking to on the phone, but also that they would still have to clean up all of the binders and folders that they had dropped all over the office when Angie told them what had happened. Plus, you should have seen the look on my mom's face when I asked her how her knee was feeling after she banged it getting out of their car."

"So, armed with that info, they had to believe your story, right?"

"Yeah, to a point. There was no denying that I knew things I probably shouldn't, but when I told them that I met our ancestors and then described who I saw, they had the same stunned look on their face that you do now. I hadn't seen any pictures of my relatives when they were older, and since they died before I was born, I really shouldn't have been able to recognize them when I saw them. I described them perfectly though, and the shock on my parent's faces let me know they had no choice but to believe my journey was more than just a dream."

The stunned look hadn't left Lou's face yet. I could see the questions flying around in his eyes as I stood up and stretched my legs out, ready to answer anything he could throw at me.

He leaned forward but stayed seated on the bench.

"Did it hurt? I mean, it had to have hurt some, right? You did basically die, so that couldn't have felt good."

"I didn't really feel anything when I actually drowned. I don't know if I was passed out and just didn't realize it, but it was almost a seamless transition. One second I was swimming under the water, the next second I was *whooshing* around with my sisters and parents while my body was under water. I am sure I might have struggled a little when I gulped in my first mouthful of water, but I really don't remember feeling any of that."

"Obviously I can't speak for everyone that has died," I continued, "but I really felt no pain. Maybe it's just my own personal belief system, but I truly believe God doesn't want any of us to suffer when we leave this life. Our souls leave our bodies before any of the real pain sets in. Know what I mean?"

"Yeah, I think so. Just trying to wrap my head around that," he said.

"You said you saw God as the Holy Trinity," he continued, "so do you think other people of other faiths go to heaven as well? I mean, it seems like obviously everything you saw and felt revolved around God, so what if they just don't believe in Him?"

"Very good question, and I've thought about that a lot. I believe that we are not here to judge each other, so who am I to say you will not make it to heaven? Although the way I was raised, Jesus clearly states '*No one can get to the Father except though me.*' I believe God loves all of His creations, no matter what their denominations might be, and I'm sure He would want all of His creation with Him. All we can do for each other is to do what Christ taught us. Love one another, be there for one another, judge not lest ye be judged. Right?"

"Yeah, that's a great way of looking at things. Everybody's personal relationship with God is their own. Whether they're really close to God or just have an on-again off-again relationship with Him is between them." He contemplated this idea. "So anyway, back to your story, you only saw a few relatives when you were there. Do you think all of your ancestors were up there in Heaven?"

"I'm not sure about that. Let me try to explain a little more. Now, maybe some of my ancestors who might not have been the nicest of people didn't go to the same place that I was. Maybe they didn't feel worthy, similarly to the way I felt when I first saw my ancestors in heaven. Maybe they kept pushing themselves away from God because of the way they hurt others here on earth. Maybe they were already judged and they are someplace else, someplace that we don't really want to think about. I don't know, but one thing is for sure. I believe that come judgment day, we will feel the love we have given others, we will feel the pain we have inflicted on others, and we will feel any emotion we may have caused others to feel."

He got quiet again with the talk of 'Judgement Day' I didn't mean it to be anything to fear. It's something we all to have to go through once our time really does come. It wasn't my time yet to sit before God and stay in Heaven, so I still have yet to have my day of judgement before my Lord. I know it's coming though, and it's a day that I am actually looking forward to when it gets here.

Looking over at Lou, I could tell he was deep in thought. His mind must have been racing, trying to get a grasp on everything that I had laid out in front of him.

"Deep in thought, huh? Thinking a little about Judgement Day? Or just thinking of how crazy I must be after hearing all this?" I was trying to lighten the mood a little, but I was also checking to see if he would say how crazy I must be.

"Like I said before, I definitely don't think you're crazy. Read the Bible, go to church, you hear about Judgement Day, but you never *really* think about what it's going to be like. I kind of pictured a big bearded guy with a list with two columns: Pros and Cons. Your good deeds and thoughts in the Pros column, and everything else in the other. Add them up and there you go. Now … with the visual in my head of that gazebo, and the bright light, and … well, everything … it all seems so much clearer now. I can actually almost picture what my own personal Judgement Day might be like. Fascinating."

"So anyway," Lou veered back to our original topic, "you were out of it for quite awhile. I bet you were chomping at the bit to tell your parents about your little trip."

"Well, after I woke up and they took the breathing tube out of my throat, I knew exactly what I wanted to say, but they gave me more medicine to make me sleep. So, it had to wait until I woke up again. When I did, my parents were still right next to my bed. I tried to sit up, and I said to them, "*I saw God!*"

I said it with such exuberance that a few people passing by on the small trail we were on glanced in our direction and smiled.

"Yeah, I think that would be a good thing to lead with." Lou laughed, not only at his little quip, but at my overly dramatic way of apparently calling attention to myself to anyone in our area.

"That's what I had wanted to say, and when I yelled that out in the hospital room, everybody looked at me funny and told me to lie down and relax. Don't get so worked up—I was going to be fine. I kept telling them, *I saw God! God loves you!* But they only seemed to brush it off and kept telling me not to talk since it was too hard on my throat."

"So you tell them you saw God after they knew you had been brain dead—is that the right term? Anyway, they knew you died. Then you woke up and said you had seen God, and they just shrugged it off as no big thing? That's a little strange."

"Yeah, I thought so too. For almost my entire life I couldn't figure out why nobody asked me any questions or wanted to hear more about my little trip. Then I found out, just a few years ago, I wasn't really talking when I was trying to tell them about God. It was nothing but gibberish coming out of my mouth. In my mind and what I had been hearing were complete and normal sentences. But apparently that's not what everybody else had heard!"

"So nobody could understand you at all?"

"Nope. I felt normal and fine, but my brain was definitely not normal and fine at that point in time. Nothing I'd said made sense for awhile after I woke up. I could understand everybody around me, but they couldn't understand me."

"Wow, that must have been a strange feeling. Awake but kind of shut off from communicating to anyone." He shook his head at the thought.

"Not only could they not understand a word I was saying, but I was basically a helpless little kid. I couldn't get up and walk because it seemed like my legs didn't know what to do. I got a ton of stuffed animals and toys while I was in the hospital. Instead of keeping them, I wanted to give them to the little kids down the hall to make them happy. I had to be pushed in a wheelchair by Angie to do it since I couldn't walk on my own. I believe, though, that children have a special connection to God, and I felt they could understand my gibberish mumbling. Every time I gave a gift to one of the kids, I would give them a hug and told them that they were very special and God loves them. I know the adults just heard some incoherent talk, but I'm pretty sure the little kids knew exactly what I was saying."

"So anyway, my brain was so scrambled at the time. I wasn't just having trouble walking, but I also couldn't remember how to feed myself. My *younger* sister had to help feed me. I kind of knew what to do, but it was like the signal from my brain to my hands was getting lost. I tried eating some Jell-O by myself, and it just kept falling off the spoon! I don't think I got one piece to my mouth. I remember laughing because I felt it was so silly and strange that I couldn't do something as easy as that. Anita had to step in and help me with that too."

I paused for a moment. For the first time since I had started this story, I could see almost a look of pity on Lou's face toward me. Maybe he was a little shocked at the events leading up to this, but he looked like he really felt sorry for me.

We walked in silence for a little while. Not even making small talk, we kept moving on down the path around the park. He was looking down most of the time, with an occasional glance over at me. We'd make eye contact, and he would just smile and look back to the flowers and trees as we passed by.

It was a perfect day outside, so there were people everywhere. Somehow though, I seriously doubted any of them were having a conversation anything similar to ours.

As we moved down a slight hill towards the small creek that ran through the park, I sensed him looking at me one more time.

"So do you still see him?" the look of pity on Lou's face had been replaced with the eager inquisitive appearance he had when I first started this tale.

"See who, God?" I knew he had more questions, but I wasn't quite sure what he meant with this one.

"No, not Him. Your guardian angel. The one that was with you when you came back, you know, the one that helped you get back into your body when you were in your hospital room. Has he made any more appearances? You think he's still around you somewhere?" Lou looked around, apparently only half joking or thinking that maybe we had some unseen company.

"Yeah, well, sort of. I believe that we each have at least two guardian angels with us at all times, so I didn't see my buddy from when I came back, but I did see one of his friends."

"We each have two? And you know what your two look like? Not sure I'd even recognize mine if they walked up to me and slapped me in the face."

"I'm sure there's more than just two protecting us. I just happen to have a pretty close relationship with two of mine. Obviously, I knew the one that came back with me. I know him as the blonde one. The one I saw later, that was the dark haired one. I'm pretty sure I saw him when I was in heaven too, but he paid a visit to me as well shortly after my return."

"You see, I was off of the tubes and machines, but I was still having some issues breathing because of a possible infection in my lungs. Anyway, I was alone in the room with just my mom at the time, and a nurse came in to check my vitals. A male nurse, if you know what I mean," I said, slightly nodding to get my point across.

"Back then there probably weren't too many male nurses, right?' Obviously, he understood exactly what I was talking about.

"Not many at all," I said. "My mom was still standing by the door when he came over to the side of my bed. He had a stethoscope and said he just wanted to give a quick listen to my breathing. I remember him being really reassuring and taking his time listening to my lungs, When he asked if I wanted to listen to my breathing as well, I turned to answer him and looked directly into his eyes. It was then I realized exactly who I was looking at."

"One of your guardian angels was there to make sure you pulled through just fine?"

"Yep, you guessed it. My dark haired protector was right there by my side. My mom was still in the room, but she obviously didn't hear a word we were saying. Actually, we weren't really *talking,* but communicating silently like we did when I had been in Heaven. He knew what I was thinking, and I apparently could *hear* exactly what he wanted me to hear."

"He asked if I was ready for my journey, and of course I said, yes. Instantly, I found myself standing in a pure white room that seemed to go on forever. The walls were glowing white, only there really weren't any walls. Just the magnificent glow of what I could only perceive to be walls. A figure slowly emerged from the glowing light, and although I couldn't really make out His face, I knew I was once again standing before my Lord."

"God? You were in front of God again?" Lou looked dumbfounded at my situation.

"I believe this time I was in the presence of Jesus. He gently put his hand on my chest and told me that I was healed. I would be whole again. I was now ready for the next part of my journey—to go back and fulfill my destiny and do His works back here on Earth."

"I reached up to give Him a hug, and just then I opened my eyes and found myself looking into the caring eyes of my angel. He wrapped his stethoscope back around his neck and stepped away from my bed. On his way out the door, he told my mom I was going to be fine, and any infection that had been in my chest was now healed. She didn't seem too happy that he appeared to 'take his time' while listening to my lungs, and rushed over to my side and asked me if I was okay. I smiled and nodding yes—I was indeed feeling perfectly fine. She spun on her heels and rushed out the door, to either give him a piece of her mind or just talk to him, not sure, but it didn't matter. When she got out into the hallway he was nowhere to be seen."

"Of course not," Lou said. "He had to get back to his day job of protecting you, right?"

"Exactly. There was a group of nurses hovering around the nursing station a few doors down from my room. Mom asked them where the male nurse disappeared to. You know what they said, right?"

"Let me guess. There were no male nurses working there."

"Well, there were male nurses at that hospital, but none working that night. Let alone working on my floor. They had no idea who my mom was talking about. Needless to say, she was more than a little confused, but when she was satisfied that I was fine, she seemed to let the whole incident go. To this day, she remembers that male nurse, but still has no real explanation for it—other than what I'd told her had happened. That wasn't the last time I actually had seen them, and I can feel them around me all the time. I know they're with me, and believe me, I am clumsy enough to keep them busy."

"So you couldn't really communicate with anyone or do even the most basic things by yourself. How long until you finally, you know, became you again?"

"Just a little while. I was able to go home from the hospital in just under a week, and I slowly got used to walking and feeding myself again, but my ability to talk normally seemed to come back all at once."

"We were at home watching TV," I continued, "and I had turned and looked at my parents and started talking about heaven."

"So you went from not talking at all, to all of a sudden talking about what you saw in heaven? That must have freaked them out." Lou looked somewhat amused at my quick vocal recovery.

"Yep, just lying on the couch when I blurted out I had seen God and started talking about heaven. They quickly turned the TV off and sat spellbound as I told them pretty much the same story I've just told you. I told them everything and answered all their questions—and believe me, they had a bunch of questions. The drowning, heaven, meeting our relatives, talking with God, I guess it's hard to hear a story like that and not have questions."

"Huh, you don't say?" Lou quickly said with a smile.

"Ha ha, real funny. Well, once I started talking I couldn't stop. I was overflowing with God's love, and I just couldn't hold it in anymore. My parents started calling me their little 'Love Child,' because I told everyone I came across that I loved them, and that God loved them more than they would ever know! I could literally feel God's love flowing through me, and I felt like I would just explode if I didn't share it with everybody that I came across."

"Love child, that's quite a nickname. Hopefully that one didn't stick around too long."

"Long enough, but it didn't really bother me. My parents were amazed at everything I was telling them, and I loved reliving the whole journey and watching the expressions on their faces as I detailed my little trip. My dad is a really visual type of guy, so he gave me a sheet of paper and asked if I was able to draw what I had seen. The angels at our house, the tunnel, the throne of God and the gazebo, I drew it all. I might have had some serious issues just a few days earlier, but it seemed as if my motor skills were coming back. I had no trouble drawing the details of my trip to Heaven. But when my dad asked me again about seeing myself in the pool, I no longer felt that overwhelming feeling of love. You remember the black, oily things that were in the pool with me?"

"Oh yeah, no way I could forget about that. The demon-type creatures, right?"

"Well, I was describing them, and I started getting a real anxious feeling and was having trouble breathing. I started to hyperventilate. My parents started freaking out thinking I was having a setback. They rushed me to the hospital, and a doctor checked me out, but by that point the feeling had subsided and I was back to my *Love Child* persona. The doctor got right up in my face and was checking my eyes and listening to my breathing, and I remember smiling at him and telling him that his breath smelled really bad, but that's okay because God still loves you!"

"First of all, not a real nice thing to say to your doctor. And second, so you freaked out talking about those demons in the pool?" I couldn't tell if Lou was joking about calling out the doctor's bad breath or not when he asked that question.

"First of all, it was all out of love telling the doctor he'd had bad breath, and everyone in the room had a big laugh with that." I smiled back at him. "And second, yeah I did freak out when I was talking about the demons. I don't know what came over me. I just had a really overwhelming feeling of dread, and it scared me so much I had a hard time breathing. By the time we got to see a doctor, I was already feeling better. I haven't had that feeling since."

"My parents explained to the doctor that just earlier in the day I'd had trouble trying to feed myself, and then all of a sudden, out of nowhere, I'd started talking again. Full sentences and making sense almost like a normal person. They wanted to know if the doctor had any idea what could have happened to flip the switch like that for me and bring me back to the world of the speaking. The doctor told them there was only one real explanation."

"That God sent you back and healed you?" Lou seemed hesitant to guess about anything that happened next in my little story, but I loved the fact that he was at least still trying.

"You're close. the doctor said, '*What happened to your daughter was a miracle. The day she woke up, all the nurses on her floor called her the miracle child, since absolutely none of them believed she would ever wake up. Obviously she's still a miracle, because I don't really see any other explanation on the sudden change in her. Just count your blessings, because she came into this hospital with a death sentence, and she's now walking out whole.*"

"Man, so you have two nicknames you can choose to go by. The Love Child or the Miracle Child. A couple of good ones, if I do say so myself."

"Yeah," I mumbled a little sheepishly. "I guess they're both kind of cool."

At this point we were coming up out of the final clearing on the path, which dumped us out at the parking lot. Our little hike was just about over, and I guess for now my storytelling would be just about over as well.

I could have continued on and told him how hard it was to be the Love Child. Don't get me wrong, I loved being filled with God's love, and I wanted to share it with everyone, but I found out that in reality, it really wasn't that easy. No longer was I the shy little kid who would have as minimal contact as possible with strangers. Nope, now, I was an outgoing little teenager that wanted to talk with everybody. I would tell every person I came across that I loved them and that God loved them more than they would ever know. While helping my parents at their work and with the vendors and customers at their flea market, it didn't matter where I was or who I was talking to. I *needed* to share with them that I had seen God and that I was filled with His love.

Some people were interested and would tell me I was wise beyond my years. Others would turn and walk away. Some even called me a freak, looking rather upset that I had just told them I loved them. I would cry and ask my parents why some people didn't want to hear that they were loved and that God is real and loves them too.

My parent's literally had to sit me down and explain that I had to try and rein it in a little. I couldn't share my story with every person I came across, and I definitely shouldn't tell complete strangers that I loved them. I was starting eighth grade soon, and I couldn't talk that way when I was at school. It made people uncomfortable, so I had to keep all that to myself.

Talk about bursting my love bubble.

My dad understood my need to share my story, though. He helped me channel it and just listen to

God. He said that my story is so special, that when somebody needed to hear it, God would bring them to me. I just had to sense what others were feeling. If I felt that I was receiving the correct cues, I would ask them if they wanted to hear what I had to say. Some people would need to hear the story to help them get through something going on in their life, while others were open enough to want to hear the whole tale. Still, others would be shut off and have no desire to hear anything about it whatsoever.

I think I read the signs right. Lou was open enough to want to hear my story—not just listen to my tale, but to also understand that this whole journey made me what I am today.

As we headed toward our cars, I could see his lips moving, but realized I hadn't heard anything he had been saying.

"What's that?" I asked. "I drifted away and didn't quite catch what you were saying."

"Drifted away huh … you feeling okay?" He was giving me a semi-serious look now.

"No, not drifting away in any type of *Epilepsy way*," if that's a thing." Just saying that out loud made me laugh. "Sharing my story made me think back to a few things. No biggie, my mind just went someplace else for a second."

"I was just saying that was an unbelievable story. Really puts some things into perspective and makes you think about what's to come. I'm sure people would love to hear your message."

"Well, like I said, not everybody is ready to hear something like this."

"True," he said, as finally approached my car. "But there are a lot of others that I think would love to hear something like that. You ever thought about writing a book?"

"Ha, yeah, the thought has crossed my mind."

PART 4...

That conversation happened close to twenty years ago now. My journey with Lou has taken us many places, and we were able to help others together. God knew what He was doing when He gave us each other.

Lou and I have been married almost seventeen years. While I've shared my story countless times in those years, rarely, if ever, have I described it as deeply as I did to him that day.

As hard as it was, I took my parent's advice from early in life and tried to 'rein in' my love child persona. It wasn't easy, but the closer I grew toward adulthood, the more I realized that some people just weren't ready to hear God's plan. As a teenager, I took it personally when somebody didn't want to hear my story, but in high school and shortly after graduation, I felt more at ease and more comfortable with knowing whom to share my journey with. If by chance the person wasn't receptive, then I knew they simply weren't ready.

I became very adept at reading people I came across and knew which part of my story and how much of it they needed to hear. It wasn't often that my path crossed with somebody that was truly ready to hear the entire journey.

Then as I moved out on my own and got a job in the 'real world,' as much as I fought against it, I seemed to always be destined to be in the customer service sector for some reason.

When, by chance, I did land a job with limited access to the public, for instance the time I spent as a graphic artist for one of our local news affiliates, it sometimes felt as if something was missing. While I enjoyed the job, I always felt I was meant for something else.

I tried new jobs periodically, from photographer to a sales manager, bartender to managing a pizza parlor, and finally a loan officer at a bank.

What do all those jobs have in common?

Constant interaction with a wide variety of people.

Don't get me wrong—there were days were I hated my job. Being on the receiving end of a customer's bad day wasn't easy. There were times when it would just wear me down.

Then I'd remember my dad's advice and tried to really read the people that would yell at me to see what the underlying issues were. I'd take a step back and think about how God put me on these people's paths for a reason.

There were more than several occasions when a customer would be very short with me and seemed annoyed even to talk to me. But there was a definite reason they were in my office interacting with me at this moment in their lives.

I would sit back and ask them the same questions. *"Are you okay? What's really going on?"*

And you would not **believe** what the people would tell me. They would open up and basically give me their entire life story.

A woman I met at a conference recently told me that her three-year old son had just passed away and she was not only questioning where her child might be now that he's gone, but also questioning her faith. She had very similar questions for God that I'd had. Why would he take her child? Why would he inflict so much pain on her and her entire family? I shut out the world, sat down next to her, and for the next hour and a half talked to her about my journey and her son. I explained how God has a plan for everything that happens here on Earth, and right now her child is living in a paradise that most people can't even imagine. Hearing my story and truly believing me when I said that I **know** that he's safe with other family members in heaven, helped ease her mind.

She said I must be an angel because it's exactly what she needed to hear at that specific moment in her life.

Now, believe me when I say that I **know** that I am no angel. I've seen angels, I know they are always with us, but I am definitely not an angel.

However, I do believe that at times they work through us, and God puts us, along with our angels, in the right place at the right time to help each other with our problems. People, like this particular lady, come into my life for a reason. That is exactly why God sent me back.

Turning my back on someone in need or in distress would be like turning my back on God Himself.

I've had grown men cry and tell me that what I shared with them changed their outlook on life, and they could understand now that there is something greater in store for them. No matter what issues or problems they were going through, God was with them. His love would help guide them through troubled times.

Random people from my parent's flea market have given me some of their personal keepsakes, because they feel so close to me after hearing about my journey. They wanted to share a little something of themselves with me as well. Most times I politely tell them I already feel a connection with them and they can keep their trinkets because I know how much these personal items must mean to them. However, other times I do accept their small gift, knowing that they might need to feel that connection in their own little way.

In the end, we all have to remember that everyone is destined to go on their own journey to paradise. Our time here on Earth is just a precursor to the amazing voyage that our souls are bound to take one day.

You don't have to have a story like mine to be able to help our fellow brother and sisters out while you're here on Earth. You don't have to have a special sense or the ability to read every person you come across.

You only have to listen.

You simply need to care.

Everybody is going through something in their lives. Sometimes they only need a friendly smile and a kind ear.

There are no coincidences in this life. God has a purpose and plan for every interaction that we have throughout the entirety of our lives, but He leaves it up to us as to decide what we do with it.

AUTHOR'S NOTE

I want to thank my mother and father (baba) for teaching me how to pray to God and for reminding me to thank Him every day that I'm still here to share His love. I believe there is no greater love then a parent's love. Thank you to my sisters, Angie and Anita, for always being that shoulder to lean on, and for being accepting of me not matter how different I may be. I want to thank my best friend Missy for allowing me to be myself and to have the deep philosophical conversation when no one understood me. You've been with me my whole life. You're my sister as well.

I also want to thank my husband Lou, for taking me by the hand and never looking back. For accepting me, encouraging me, and most importantly, for loving me. God made you perfect for me. I know that no matter what comes our way, we always have each other. Even though we never had children of our own; we are blessed with so many nephews and nieces to love as our own. Our journey has been amazing.

Most of all, thank you to God. You saw that I was a selfish and stubborn teenage girl who doubted you at times. You yanked me out of this world to show me that we are all together in this journey that we call life. You gave me a clear purpose, and there is no greater purpose than to serve God. You showed me how much unconditional love You have for all of us and how we should share it.

I may be older now, but that young love child is still within me. So to anyone else that is reading this right now, I hope you will always remember this.

I LOVE YOU.

CPSIA information can be obtained
at www.ICGtesting.com
Printed in the USA
BVOW07s0220020318
509538BV00017B/239/P